Design a Baltimore Album Quilt!

A TEACH-YOURSELF COURSE IN SETS AND BORDERS

A DESIGN COMPANION TO
BALTIMORE BEAUTIES AND BEYOND,
STUDIES IN CLASSIC ALBUM QUILT APPLIQUÉ
VOLUME II

by Elly Sienkiewicz

C&T PUBLISHING

Copyright ©1992 Eleanor Patton Hamilton Sienkiewicz
Edited by Sayre Van Young, Berkeley, California
Technical editing by Joyce Lytle, San Ramon, California
Design, illustration, and production coordination by Julie Olson,
Olson Design and Illustration, Washington, DC
Additional illustrations by Rose Sheifer, Graphic Productions,
Walnut Creek, California

Acknowledgments: Thank you to all of you who helped make this book possible.
No ordinary words do justice to my appreciation.

Front Cover Photo: Sarah Shaefer Album Quilt, mid-nineteenth century.
(Photo courtesy of America Hurrah Quilts and Antiques, NYC)

Front Cover Border: Updegraf Feather Border. This design is based on the Updegraf
Album Quilt (inscribed, in part, "Baltimore" and "1850"), Quilt #8
in *Baltimore Beauties and Beyond, Volume II.*

Nineteenth-century clip art from these Dover publications: *Hands: A Pictorial Archive from
Nineteenth-Century Sources* (1985); *Harter's Picture Archive for Collage and Illustration* (1978);
Victorian Spot Illustrations, Alphabets, & Ornaments from Porret's Type Catalog (1982).

Published by C&T Publishing
P.O. Box 1456
Lafayette, California 94549

ISBN: 0-914881-57-4

Library of Congress Card No.: 92-33103

Sienkiewicz, Elly.
    Design a Baltimore album quilt! : a teach-yourself course in sets
and borders / by Elly Patton Hamilton Sienkiewicz.
        p. cm.
    ISBN 0-914881-57-4 : $18.95
    1. Appliqué—Patterns. 2. Album quilts—Maryland—Baltimore.
3. Patchwork—Patterns. I. Title.
TT779.s543   1992
746.44'5—dc20

First Edition
Printed in the United States of America
10 9 8 7 6 5 4 3 2 1

Contents

PHOTO 1. BALTIMORE ALBUM REDONE.
1986-1988. 95½" x 95½". The East Bay Heritage Quilters' elegant reproduction of the Metropolitan Museum of Art's mid-nineteenth-century Baltimore-style Album Quilt. That antebellum original reflects the epitome of the famous Baltimore Album style. Gloriously bright and equally beautiful, this contemporary group-made version meets such a uniformly high standard that one might suspect a single maker. Above all its other aesthetic accomplishments, it is the set of the antique Album that, in a comparison of these quilts, draws our admiration. There seems to have been a purposeful evolution in Album Quilt sets from equal-sized blocks, set together and bordered, to this impressive set where block size gradations create both a medallion center and self-borders, all in a perfect harmony of proportion. *(Photo courtesy of Sharon Risedorph)*

Introduction

The number of "Baltimore Beauties" is mushrooming. Certain of these revivalist Albums stand out. Their unique style and flair echoes the antebellum Albums. This kind of needleart in its old age often ends up in museums or being traded with high visibility at auction. The question is, how do quiltmakers create Album Quilts that are celebrated down the centuries as outstanding? How do they design a showcase, a setting? The quiltmakers must be as familiar with the classic set style as they are with the diverse block styles themselves.

Design a Baltimore Album Quilt! is a teach-yourself course in classic sets and borders. Whether we study this course alone or with others, we'll improve our skills and steep ourselves in the collective insights of bygone Baltimore. It should provide simple, practical answers about set. And for some it may guide their modern quilts to classic heights.

We quiltmakers working in the revivalist Baltimore style seek intimate familiarity with that style. It is impractical, though, to actually set numbers of these quilts together. This workbook, however, provides a workable and easy solution. It allows us to set multiple quilts together, quickly and easily, on paper. By so doing we should become so well versed in our set options that we can exercise them with an almost intuitive ease.

This workbook was written to help us tackle how to set these beautiful blocks together. Because we can never have seen all the quilts of the classic Album style, no book can pretend to be definitive. Moreover, a book inevitably reflects the author's personal taste. Please keep this in mind, for your taste, your sense of style, are the final word. If you love a look I haven't lauded, go for it! Even if we have little confidence in our own taste, but are nevertheless encouraged to pursue what we like, the possibility exists that we'll do something wonderful. I've always appreciated a college studio art professor who just stood and looked for a few minutes every day at my work, but made no comment. I was absorbed in painting our assignment, a potted teak plant. Exaggerating the sinuous grace of the leaf-shapes gave me pleasure. Playing with color, splitting the leaves with white space and painting each half a different color, mixing my favorites, wantonly, throughout, found me happily lured on—the willing follower of some primitive muse. On the last day, the professor said, "Oh, now I see what you're doing. I didn't know before. Nice." If he had sounded critical before I'd finished, I suspect I would not have had the confidence to continue listening to that muse. In the end, I really liked it. Even he liked it. (I was told my painting disappeared from the art closet after our class exhibition. And in that, I suppose, could be the supreme compliment!)

In *Design a Baltimore Album Quilt!*, I have tried to analyze a set style and explain why certain antique quilts in this style seem particularly memorable. Yours is to emulate old Baltimore, or to take the potential of this classic style far beyond its nineteenth-century flowering. I hope these lessons introduce you to the myriad possibilities of traditional Album block sets in the Baltimore mode. And then I hope they encourage you to do it your way.

Picture this:

Quilter's Solitaire (An Introductory Simile)
Think of your quilt blocks as playing cards. You have a handful of cards. They have two "faces." On one face they are all alike. Turn them over to the reverse face and they are all different. (See A and B.) Liken this to a collection of Album Quilt blocks that are all alike in their size and shape and background color. But their other face, the design and color pattern, is quite different from block to block.

In learning how to arrange your cards (and your quilt blocks), try to become familiar with just one face, one aspect, at a time. Try to visualize these aspects as two separate design variables. Once you are conversant with your design options, then you can mix a bit of this and that from them with abandon!

Lay out sixteen of your cards in a pattern, like a quilt block set, all with the same face up. (See C.) Because each block is the same as the next, this set is restful (almost boring here). If the cards were laid with their diverse faces up, this tight set might have quite the opposite affect. It would seem random and quite distracting because the design patterns on the cards are all different. Mightn't we also have that problem with different Album blocks set too tightly together?

Now set the cards with an equal amount of white space running between each card. (See D.) This adds another element to our card design and has a nice, restful symmetry to it. The added white space created by the white sashing would certainly rest the eye between complex blocks too. Let's take that variable, spacing, and set up a slightly more complex, potentially more interesting pattern. (See E.)

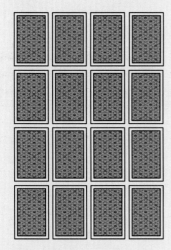

A. Considered from one aspect, your appliqué blocks are all different.

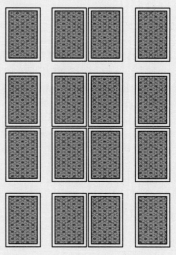

B. Looked at another way, your blocks are all the same.

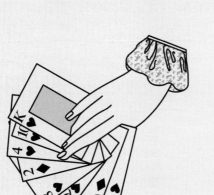

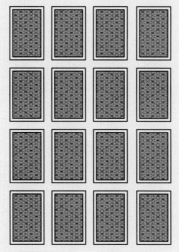

C. In quilt terms, this is called "4 x 4 set block to block."

D. In a quilt, we would call this "4 x 4 set with sashing."

E. 4 x 4 set with a central cross shape to the blocks because of the four intersecting rows of sashing.

Ponder this:

Taking just this one variable, spacing, we could devise lots of pleasing patterns for arranging our same-faced cards. Are you ready for a bit of "Quilter's Solitaire"? Take your playing cards and see what sets you can come up with, pushing your spacing option to add zest to 3 x 3, 4 x 4, 5 x 5, and 6 x 6 block sets.

If a given set particularly appeals to you, turn the cards over. Do you need something stronger to hold the total design together, now that each card has a different face? What new variables will you have to consider with the diverse card designs showing?

Try keeping the same set, but rearrange the cards within the set with the aim of achieving a more pleasing presentation. Consider quilt block design variables such as color, density of design, or complexity of design as the rationale for how you come up with your new card set scheme. Your card game has introduced you, conceptually, to many of the basic issues of setting Album blocks together. And wasn't it easy?

Victorian Peacock Feather Fan
Like the flowers in the Album Quilts, fans had their own symbolic Victorian language, part of which was in the arrangement of the fan and in its presentation. Victorian maidens used the fan as a flirtatious device, one more artful intricacy in an era whose style was dominated by eclecticism, whose key characteristic is elaborateness, and whose favorite adjective was "elegant."

Read on. These Beauties are more than willing to share their artful secrets with us if we will but focus our attentions upon them. From a fan of cards, to a fan of peacock feathers, to a block collection of memorable beauty, the closer acquaintance of those fascinating ladies of bygone Baltimore will teach us. The Baltimore-style Album Quilt sets the standard and remains our inspiration.

Title Abbreviations

For brevity, the following abbreviations are used to refer to my Album Quilt book titles in the text that follows:

- *Spoken Without a Word* = Spoken Without a Word—A Lexicon of Selected Symbols, with 24 Patterns from Classic Baltimore Album Quilts

- *Volume I* = Baltimore Beauties and Beyond, Studies in Classic Album Quilt Appliqué, Volume I

- *Volume I, Pattern Companion* = Baltimore Album Quilts, Historic Notes and Antique Patterns—A Pattern Companion to Baltimore Beauties and Beyond, Studies in Classic Album Quilt Appliqué, Volume I

- *Volume II* = Baltimore Beauties and Beyond, Studies in Classic Album Quilt Appliqué, Volume II

- *Design a Baltimore Album Quilt!* = Design a Baltimore Album Quilt! A Teach-Yourself Course in Sets and Borders—A Design Companion to Baltimore Beauties and Beyond, Studies in Classic Album Quilt Appliqué, Volume II

- *Dimensional Appliqué* = Dimensional Appliqué—Baskets, Blooms, and Baltimore Borders—A Pattern Companion to Baltimore Beauties and Beyond, Studies in Classic Album Quilt Appliqué, Volume II

- *Volume III* = Baltimore Beauties and Beyond, Studies in Classic Album Quilt Appliqué, Volume III

PHOTO 2. ALBUM QUILT.

Mid-nineteenth century. 100" x 104". This is a strong, simple set with a red print border that echoes the sashing. The challenge in any Album quilt is to frame a diversity of blocks and to present them prettily. Certainly this graphic quilt meets that challenge well. Note the three link chains (the Oddfellow symbol for "friendship, love, and truth") at one basket's rim; at the base of another basket may be a pair of gavels (the symbolic tool by which we chip off our "rough edges" in seeking the moral perfection symbolized by a square). In another block we see the symbolic heart and hand ("service and the spirit in which it is given"). Yet another heart and hand block is full of obvious fraternal symbols. (*Photo courtesy of Abby Aldrich Rockefeller Folk Art Center*)

Part One: Getting Started

So many of us have come to regard our Album blocks as heirlooms in themselves. Taking the next step of setting them into an Album quilt, where the whole will be even more breathtaking than the sum of its parts, can be intimidating. By working step-by-step through the lessons in this hands-on manual, you'll find the set style that pleases you most, and you'll explore numerous design possibilities.

Beyond design experience, this workbook teaches practical skills like making a Master Border Pattern and a Master Border Corner Pattern, customizing border motifs, and attaching blocks, sashings, and borders. It also discusses quilting and unique bindings. The lessons offer simple eye-opening exercises, taught through a series of quick and easy pencil, paper, and paste exercises.

By doing the exercises, you'll understand how to use borders, sashing, directional blocks, white space, block design density, interior pattern, and medallion centers. And, you'll quickly feel more confident about selecting the right set, border, and finishing touches for your masterpiece.

Wherever you are in the block-making process, you're on your way to an heirloom Album Quilt. Simply learning the richness of this style has been an adventure. As you've worked on one pattern, you've enjoyed thinking ahead to which block you want to do next. (These Albums, these "collections on a theme," excite the collecting passion in each of us.) Meanwhile, you're learning much more than needlework—you're making the acquaintance of an expressive quilt genre. You've discovered that you're able to make any of the classic blocks, from simple to complex. It simply takes patience. And you're in no rush. You're steeped in the process and the beauty it promises. These Album squares are something to dream on. Inevitably, though, your thoughts turn towards the final set, the finished quilt.

Why study sets before you have all your blocks made? One good reason is to leave yourself open to a change of plan as your knowledge expands. After all, a baby or wall quilt can be as few as four blocks and a bed quilt as few as nine blocks (see Quilts #13 and #17 in *Volume II*). But for many of us, we need to learn more, collect more blocks, ease ourselves back into the Victorian sensibilities of this mode, and savor it. Even so, take a bit of time, now, and do a few easy lessons on sets and borders, then go back to sewing. What you've learned by doing the first exercises will sit at the back of your mind. Visions of sets will slip into your daydreams. This seems a necessary part of the quiltmaking process.

Sometimes you'll be drawn to a set that needs a particular type of block, and you can sew towards filling those needs. Others of you will find that you've grown as you've worked in the Album style. Your color and design tastes have become more defined. At this point, you may see that you are really working on two quilts. One is the full-sized quilt that has evolved in your mind. Another is a smaller quilt, say four- or nine-block, that takes its inspiration from the squares selected out from the larger quilt. Now, some ten years into this Album Quilt revival, I have to admit to pleasure when I hear that two quilts are being worked on. It seems a measure of how far we've come, to want something more than a housing for all the blocks we've made. We seem to have reached classic heights ourselves, when we can take these wondrously diverse patterned squares and use them as building blocks in a greater whole.

I. Course Goals

When I was a school teacher (now so many years ago), we had to make weekly Lesson Plans that included our goals for those lessons. Since this is a teach-yourself course, let's set some goals.

Goal #1: Meet classic sets and their design variables

Happily, this book's scope is limited. (Happily, because the possibilities of setting blocks together into traditional quilt form are multitudinous!) It concentrates on the somewhat limited range of known classic Album Quilt sets. My first goal is to familiarize you with these classic sets. Those of us who'd like to emulate the style associated with old Baltimore need the same close familiarity with the details of its sets that we've acquired about the diversity of its blocks.

To begin with, from what vantage point did that Baltimorean needlewoman envision this quilt she was setting-out? In those antebellum Albums, many quilts, but perhaps not most, have blocks assembled as we might have in our own sampler quilts a decade or two ago. At that time we wanted to make a balanced collection (an Album) of blocks that differed significantly one from another. Chances are we laid these blocks on the floor or pinned them to a wall. Most of us envisioned the finished quilt displayed at a quilt show, or full-face on the page of a magazine. In our late-twentieth-century quilt revival, the minority seem to picture their sampler quilts as they would lie over a bed.

Just the reverse of this seems true in the classic Albums. Most of those seem designed with the bed site, rather than a hung position, uppermost in the quilt-maker's mind. (Perhaps this explains why most blocks are placed right-side up as you would approach the bed from different directions. Occasionally there is a bit of confusion to this scheme—or perhaps the inexplicable turn of a corner block is that fabled "humility block" that defies perfection from the hand of man.) How and where you see the quilt displayed is among the set choices, now yours to make.

Introducing the Design Variables of Classic Sets: First, what is a design variable? Here, a "variable" is anything changeable in the design of the set. Some of these variables are external to the blocks. And some are within the blocks themselves. Surprisingly, for all their richness, the familiar classic Albums use just a fraction of all the sets that could yield a traditional quilt. You'll get to know the classic Albums in the section on quilt set models in Part Two, and by studying the quilts referred to in the accompanying text. But you may also see untried possibilities as you experiment with the sets provided there. All sorts of sets are diagrammed in this workbook. Think of as many variables involved in a set as possible. The variables that follow are your design options.

1. *Size of the block* (Block size is usually uniform, but some may be enlarged to form rectangles or over-sized squares. Some classic Baltimore Album Quilts employed an "enlarged center block and side rectangle" set. An already famous reproduction of this set can be seen in Photo 1.)

2. *Position the blocks are set in* (Blocks may be set in horizontal rows, or diagonal rows, or set concentrically around a center.)

3. *How the blocks are set in relation to each other* (Set together without sashing, or with sashing, or with piping or blank blocks between, or separated by borders.)

4. *Whether the finished quilt is square or rectangular* (Most classic Albums are square.)

5. *Whether the width of the quilt has an odd or even number of blocks* (Odd numbers (3, 9, 25) have a natural center block. If even numbers (4, 16, 36) of blocks are to have a center focus, it must be created by enlarging the center blocks, or by repeating a pattern on the center blocks. Blocks can be repeated exactly, as in Quilt #7 in *Volume I*, or their general effect can be repeated. An example of the latter is the repeated building blocks that center Quilt #2 in *Volume I, Pattern Companion*.)

6. *Nature of the sashing* (Same fabric as the block's background, or a color, or a large chintz print, or a bold border stripe, or pieced, or appliquéd, and with or without corner blocks.)

7. *Homogeneity of the blocks* (Similar palette, similar density.)

8. *Differences in the appliqué's overall shape on the block* (Used to advantage to produce internal pattern.)

9. *Presence or absence of a border*

10. *Nature of the border* (Borders can differ in width or color; in cloth: plain or print; in method: pieced or appliquéd. Borders can be all the same or differ from one quilt side to the other.)

11. *Border corners* (Are they a continuation of the border motif or something significantly different? Do the borders open up the quilt's corners, or do they close them off?)

12. *Binding and edging treatment* (These can be particularly effective design elements.)

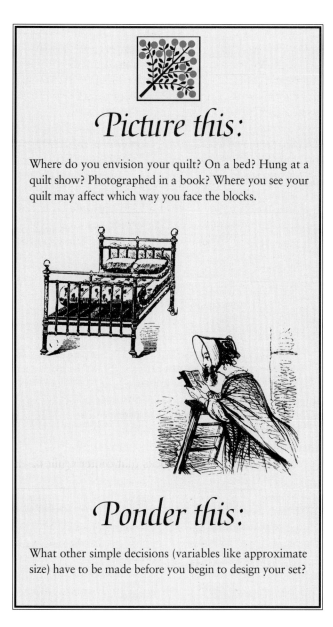

Picture this:

Where do you envision your quilt? On a bed? Hung at a quilt show? Photographed in a book? Where you see your quilt may affect which way you face the blocks.

Ponder this:

What other simple decisions (variables like approximate size) have to be made before you begin to design your set?

2. *Any border, even a white (background color) border helps unify a quilt.* (See Photo 4-8 in *Volume II.*)

3. *White (or negative) space is powerful.* A consistent amount of white space surrounding the block's pattern helps unify a quilt. In some quilts this is achieved by piecing the blocks together with white sashing. (See Photos 4-9 and 4-27 in *Volume II.*)

4. *The background fabric (which reads as one color) is itself an important element in unifying the quilt.* One of the conventions of classic Album Quilt design is to have one background color throughout the quilt. Occasionally a block or border will carry a tiny print, or be off-color by a shade or two. These anomalies add richness to a background that basically reads as one color.

5. *A bold sashing is an excellent way to unify a quilt.* It can be as simple as strips of calico. (See Photo 4-28 in *Volume II.*) Or it can be a strong pieced sashing like the garden maze of Quilt #7 or the diamond sashing of Quilts #2, 4, and 17 in that book. Even the narrow appliquéd chains seen in quilts like Photo 4-22 (*Volume II*, again) bind with surprising strength.

6. *The combination of a strong border and a medallion center presents almost any diversity of blocks as a cohesive quilt.*

7. *Graduated scale (center block enlarged fourfold, edged by doublesize blocks, bordered by single blocks) can make the outer row of blocks function effectively as a border.* Perhaps because of its remarkable success, this combination is repeated in multiple quilts. This set reached its peak in the style seen in Photo 1.

Goal #2: Get acquainted with the external elements that can unify diverse block

What binds all these elements into not only a cohesive but a beautiful whole? In a group quilt, for example, where the selection of blocks is already a given, you need an external element to unify the quilt:

1. *Sometimes a very strong border unifies the quilt beautifully.* See, for example, Photo 4-14 in *Volume II.* In that classic Baltimore Album Quilt, a block-wide serpentine feather-plume border holds 36 quite disparate blocks together in an elegant whole. There is no sophisticated internal pattern of squares here: the blocks all face the foot of the bed and are placed in six horizontal rows. Individually, some blocks are simple, while some are wondrously intricate. It is the border itself that frames this block collection into a magnificently cohesive quilt.

Goal #3: Learn an easy method for designing sets and choosing borders

Simply put, the method of this book entails cutting up black-and-white pictures of blocks and borders and pasting them (with a repositionable adhesive) into printed quilt diagrams.

This design approach teaches a lot about sets and borders. The traditional alternative is cumbersome: to play with the blocks themselves and imagine them in borders. One step beyond that is to arrange snapshots of your blocks, like playing cards, and make a fabric mock-up of a border segment to aid your visualization. Keep this method in mind as a way of doublechecking your black-and-white design. The exciting point is that an awful lot can be learned (quickly and easily) by doing a black-and-white mock-up of a Baltimore-style Album Quilt.

Our method here assumes that your squares, like the

Picture this:

You hold the cards. Any one of these cards, or any combination of them, is at your fingertips. They are yours to use and they hold the key to your quilt's future!

Ponder this:

Are there any missing cards? What other design variables might be included in our list of changeable quilt factors?

classic Albums themselves, share a reasonably consistent palette. Thus color (geared to your taste) can be saved until last, to strengthen a set and border design that has been arrived at in black and white. Furthermore, working out the set of the blocks themselves without color reinforces the importance of the less obvious factors in an Album's set. These include the shape of the appliqué on the square, and the density of the appliqué. The proportion of positive (appliqué) space to negative (background cloth) is important to the block's overall appearance.

Making a paper quilt mock-up can help answer more specific questions as well. For example, does it make sense to design the set of the blocks themselves before you consider borders? Are there circumstances where it would be best to choose the border early on in the process?

II. Supplies

To do the exercises that accompany each lesson, you'll need the following items:

1. Your *Baltimore Beauties* books and other pictures of Baltimore-style Album Quilts

2. Good paper scissors, pencil, ruler, and graph paper

3. Repositionable glue-stick and repositionable transparent tape (available at your stationers or art supply store). It's important to use a repositionable adhesive so your charts can be used over and over.

4. Envelopes for storing your cut-and-paste graphics cut from the pull-out Pattern Resource Sheet.

III. How to Use This Book

Level I. This book provides the necessary ingredients for making pasted mock-ups of appliqué Album Quilt sets. These include blank quilt-set diagrams, representative classic Baltimore Album Quilt blocks, border frame diagrams, and printed strips of borders. The pull-out Pattern Resource Sheet reproduces a number of the blocks and border strips in this book. Cut up this Pattern Resource Sheet to paste Album Quilt design mock-ups. Keep the separate blocks and borders sorted by storing them in labeled envelopes. To do an exercise, choose the blocks and/or borders that please you, and paste them directly into the book.

A great deal can be learned about classic set characteristics, just by penciled symbols on graph paper or by this cut-and-paste design method. Level II suggests a convenient way to go beyond this workbook. Level III recognizes the beauty of Album Quilt set styles and envisions your "paper appliqué" Album design as frameable art.

Level II. To aid further study, you can combine this workbook with other resources for a "working file" of design ideas. Have this workbook hole-punched (your copier store does this for a couple of dollars) and set into a three-ring binder. Include Album photos, magazine clippings, extra graph paper (to record all your design mockups or to do additional ones), and additional photocopies of your favorite quilt-set diagrams, blocks, and borders. That way you can preserve all your mock-ups and still re-use your favorite design elements as you work your way through the exercises.

Remember, the proportions in most of these diagrams (block= 1", sashing =1/8", border = 5/8") are roughly equivalent to many of the quilt photographs in the *Baltimore Beauties* series. Thus you can cut apart photocopies from these books for inclusion in your mock-ups. After you've worked the block lessons, you may want to work with pictures of the actual blocks you've made or plan to make. Photo-reduce these blocks (or their pictures) from the books to the mock-up size.

Level III. The Paper Album. For many years, print-maker/quiltmaker Judy Severson has printed traditional-style quilts on fine paper and embossed these frameable prints (on cards and posters) with beautiful quilting designs. Her recent works reflect her interest in the appliqué Album Quilts. They show the fruits of her exploration of set style. Two of her print-quilts are included in this book.

Photographs, watercolors, and prints are all ways to enjoy quilt images as frameable art. Another is to make your mock-ups out of fabric fused to paper. To do this, cut the elements of the quilt (blocks, sashings, borders, binding) out of fabric backed with a fusible web. Then fuse them to paper. Work with 3" to 4" blocks (or larger). And be sure to use excellent scissors (embroidery or 5" tailor point).

The Miniature Album. Some remarkably exquisite Albums have been made and will surely be included among the next century's heirlooms. Because of sheer number of stitches taken, simplifying and miniaturizing a large Album block down to 6" or less would speed the final quilt. It's well understood, though, that quicker in this case by no means implies easier! The smaller the scale, the more difficult it is to do fine, intricate appliqué. Unless you do what Darlene Scow did on her exquisite miniature shown in the Color Section of *Volume I*. She hand button-hole finished fused cut-outs of the appliqué shapes. (For instructions on how to hand finish fused appliqué, see method #5 in *Appliqué 12 Easy Ways!*) For a slightly less awe-inspiring look, one could machine blanket-stitch the raw edge.

The enthusiasm poured forth from all of you who have read and sewn by these books is really remarkable. Sometimes I imagine that a contingent of nineteenth-century Album quiltmakers appears at one of our "Show and Tells." After the initial shock, I imagine how close they and we would feel to each other, how well we would understand each other. I'm sure there would be lots of warm laughter, and excited exchanges of technical information, and wonderful quilts to see. I believe so much of the social patterns of what we do, and our earnestness, would be familiar to them. As one insightful quiltmaker said at a recent national conference, "No one ever asks you what you do at these things. They all know the important thing about you: You quilt." And if nonquilters knew the depth of what that simple statement bespeaks, they might well envy us.

PHOTO 3. SARAH McILWAIN'S QUILT.

Mid-nineteenth century. 94" x 94". As delightfully informal as others are formal, the symbols and block patterns in this quilt tie it closely to those in documentable Baltimore Album Quilts. The Mexican War Memorial (block C-4) looks much like that inscribed "Ringgold" in Quilt #1 in the Color Section, and the berry-laden wreathed hearts so often seen near memorials anchor this quilt's corners. Sarah McIlwain almost surely was a Rebekah, proudly displaying her badge sash in block C-2. Her quilt delights in symbols, appliquéing them on blocks, borders, sashings with abandon. For us, studying sets and borders, the sprinkled motifs of the sashings and diminutive odd-lot blocks of the border may, along with Sarah's hand-holding figures and proud title, free us up and give us ideas! (*Photo ©1989 courtesy of Sotheby's, Inc., New York*)

Part Two: The Lessons

These Lessons are for making the intimate acquaintance of classic Album Quilt sets and borders. The lessons are divided into three sections: Quilt Set Models (including sashings), Blocks and Medallions, and Borders. Each has a resource section and graphics for doing the exercises. By doing the lessons, you'll be using the concepts you've just read about. The graphics in each section repeat and refer to the block set diagrams, blocks, and borders throughout. (You may want to flag the pages where these three graphic sources are.) The pull-out Pattern Resource Sheet repeats material from the book so you can cut and paste it to the set models. Reproduce more copies, as needed, from the book itself.

I. Quilt Set Models

Introduction to Block Sets. Nine-, sixteen-, and twenty-five-block sets (plus the occasional larger or smaller one) are the block sets modeled on the following pages. We're concentrating here on sets for which an antebellum example exists. Because rectangular quilts were rare in this style, we've only shown those with an antique quilt precedent.

Your basic choices are to set the block square, or to set the block on point. Next you have to decide whether to set the blocks right next to each other, or to place sashing strips between (and even around) them. Sashing strip models come later in this section. First, let's see what our options are for setting the squares. These set diagrams are based on the scale of 1" square per block, 1/8" wide for most sashing, and 5/8" wide for most classic borders. (Some revivalist Baltimore borders pictured in Section III will be 1" wide.) These proportions are

roughly those of the quilts photographed throughout the *Baltimore Beauties* series. This means you could cut up photocopies of those photos to use their designs in your mock-ups. A few quilt examples from the *Baltimore Beauties* series are cited in parentheses. Noting how often certain set-style details are repeated will help you understand the genre better. Note: While some antebellum quilts don't have borders, for simplicity all our diagrams do.

A. Blocks Set Square Without Sashing:
Quilt Set Models 1 through 4

Two interior designs show up with some frequency in 5 x 5 quilts set without sashing. One (Figure 1A) is a Greek, or Maltese, or Templar's Cross that's anchored by dense blocks at the compass points next to the border. (See Quilt #2 in *Volume I.*) Another pattern we see a lot of (Figure 1B) forms a diamond shape. This square-on-point made of eight open wreaths around a short-armed cross seems sought after in the classic quilts. In fact, in the most successful examples of this set, every other block is an open wreath. (See Quilt #9 in *Volume II.*) Often, this cross centers on the dove and book, or the eagle and flag with various generosities (sprays, wreaths, garlands, baskets) of flowers adorning them. Closest to this center block are containers (epergnes, urns, cornucopias, but most often baskets) of the earth's blessings: fruits, flowers, nuts.

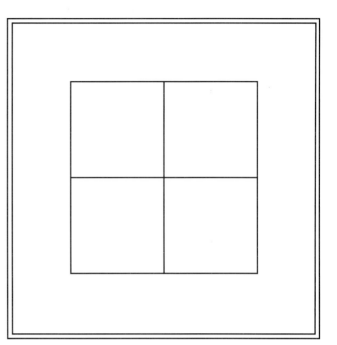

Quilt Set Model 1.
Four blocks (2 x 2) set square
without sashing and bordered.

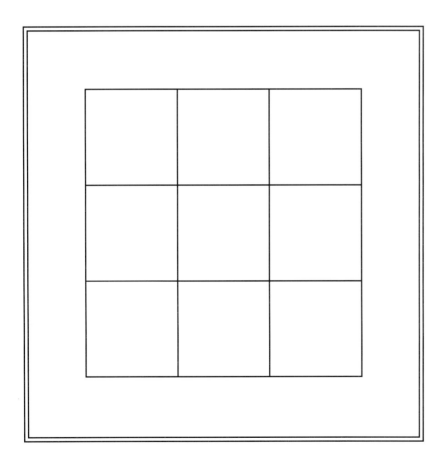

Quilt Set Model 2.
Nine blocks (3 x 3) set square
without sashing and bordered.

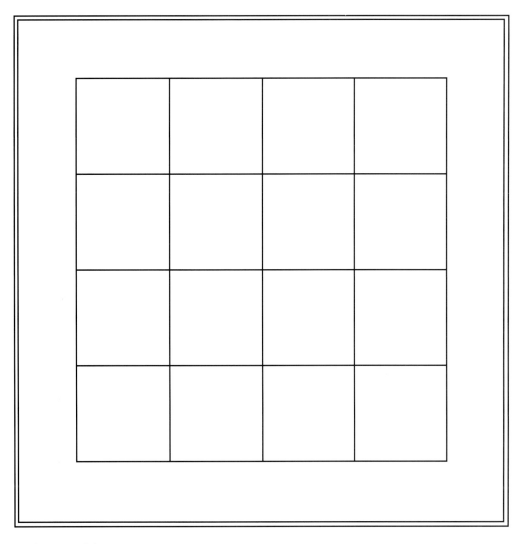

Quilt Set Model 3.
Sixteen blocks (4 x 4) set square
without sashing and bordered.

Color itself can also draw attention in a quilt. Look over the color sections in your *Baltimore Beauties* series, and see how often the urns and epergnes are blue, the baskets are red (with touches of blue and yellow), and cornucopias repeat three linked chains of red, blue, and yellow. The colors stand out from all the greenery in these floral Albums.

Yet a third interior pattern (Figure 1C) could be created by contrasting it with the three blocks in each corner. I don't recognize this set in the antique Albums, but it seems full of possibilities. A fourth set, an unnamed cross, was made of predominantly red blocks in a contemporary Album, Quilt #6 in *Volume I*. It is outlined in Figure 1D.

The nine center squares are prominently displayed on the bed, so the showiest blocks can be found here. Consider these nine centered squares carefully. Ornate blocks often have more white space around the design. Presumably this is because the appliqué has shrunk the pattern area a bit. More white space is very effective in drawing attention to a particular block. It also emphasizes the pattern set up by a number of such blocks. In one elegant Victorian Album, six of these blocks form a Roman cross. (See Figure 1E.)

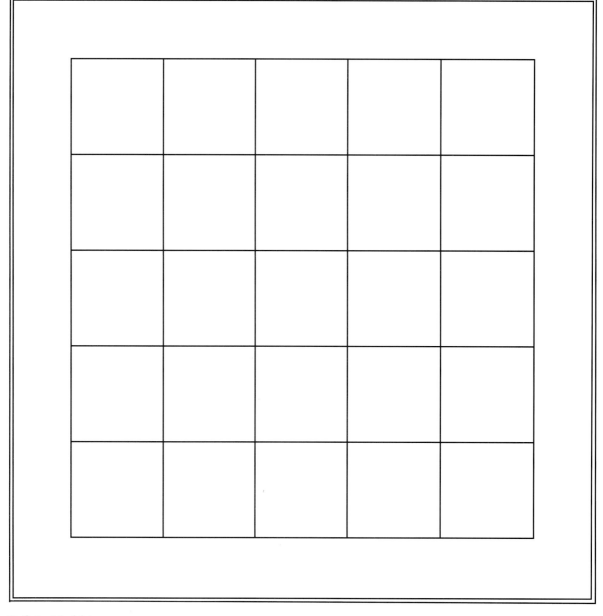

Quilt Set Model 4.
Twenty-five blocks (5 x 5) set square
without sashing and bordered.

Blocks Set Square with Sashing:
Quilt Set Models 5 through 7

"Sashing" is the fabric rectangles used to frame the blocks. Sashing spaces the blocks. It can be the same color as the block's background fabric and simply serve to add more "white space." Or it can be ornamental with color, a print, some piecing, or appliqué. When highly visible, the sashing stops the eye and frames each block. I find the use of sashing comforting because it separates diverse blocks and makes the designing of group quilts easier for me. I love the look of blocks set without sashing or with background color sashing, but they seem to demand more careful block placement.

They also require more detail and excitement in the quilting pattern. (See Photo 4-27 in *Volume II.*) Graphically strong sashing can also unify diverse blocks in a well defined all-over grid. (See Photo 4-22 and Photo 4-31 in *Volume II.*) For simplicity, on the diagrams we've made our sashing run between all the blocks. Then we've carried the same sashing around the outside boundary of the body of blocks where they touch the border. (See Photos 4-31, 4-32, and 4-33 in *Volume II.*) In many antique Albums, though, the sashing ran between all blocks, but not between the blocks and the borders. (See Photos 4-23, 4-27, and 4-28 in *Volume II.*)

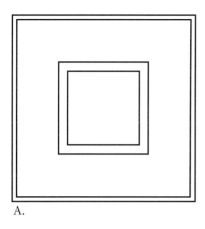

A.

Quilt Set Model 5.
A. One block set square with sashing.
B. One block set square with sashing, then set within a square on point and then within a square set square. This is an effective way of making a one-block quilt into a much more substantial quilt. (See Photo 4-4 in *Volume II*.)

B.

Figure 1A-E. Interior Patterns. The gray highlights "interior patterns" that can be set up within a quilt. Designs can be made within the body of the quilt by careful selection and placement of the blocks. Like sets themselves, there are a wealth of possibilities, many untried. As you do the lesson exercises, you'll appreciate how ingeniously interior designs have been used in the antique Albums.

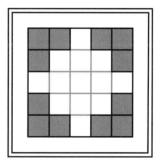

Interior Pattern C.
Three blocks that read as dense in the three corner blocks should throw the focus on a more open interior design. Or you could reverse the experiment.

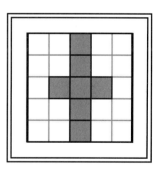

Interior Pattern D.
Cross pattern in a contemporary Album (Quilt #6 in *Volume I*) designed by the author.

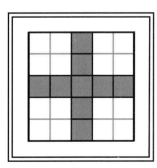

Interior Pattern A.
Short-armed cross (the Greek, Maltese, or Templar's cross).

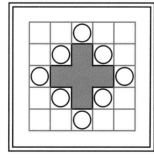

Interior Pattern B.
Square-on-point medallion of eight wreaths around a center short-armed cross.

Interior Pattern E.
Roman Cross made of ornate blocks whose design has more white space around it than the surrounding blocks.

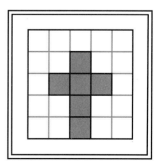

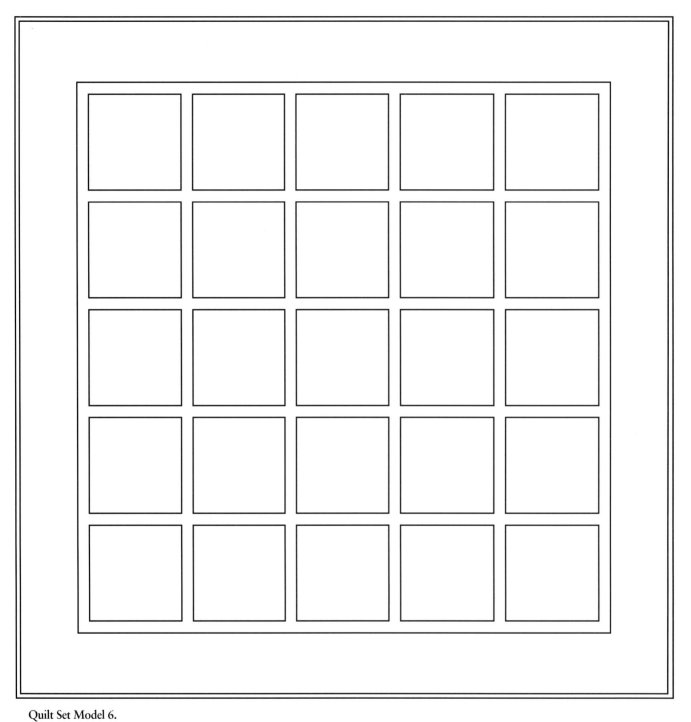

Quilt Set Model 6.

Twenty-five blocks (5 x 5) set square with sashing and bordered. This set has a natural center. It is probably the most common classic Album set. Photo 4-19 in *Volume II,* for example, shows a dramatic quilt with an exceptionally finely scaled *scheren-* *schnitte* block at its center. The oft-seen Maltese or Greek Cross radiates to the compass points from this center. See how it is formed by "weaker" or less space-filling blocks in between the arms of the cross.

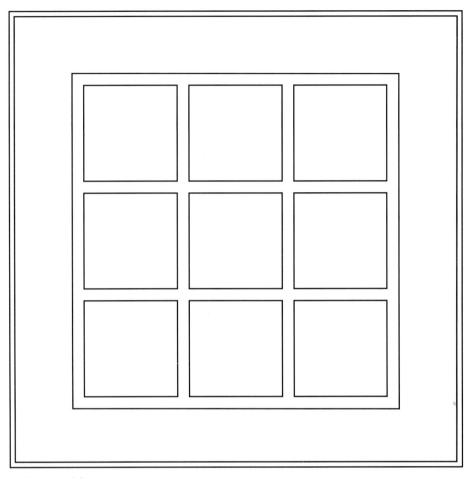

Quilt Set Model 7.

Nine blocks (3 x 3) set square with sashing and bordered.
The Odense Album (Quilt #17 in *Volume II*) is an interesting version of this set. Its four corner blocks are placed on the diagonal and point towards the center. The center block is a medallion, not because it is enlarged, but because it is small. Thus, the white space surrounding it is enlarged. By a rather spectacular accident, the border I designed on paper (appliquéd exquisitely by Albertine Veenstra) echoes the center and wraps the whole in a spinning circle. If one wanted to, one could probably make a circle ripple (like ripples caused by pebbles tossed in a pond) through concentric rows of a twenty-five-block quilt. I can imagine four red urns with dipping curved rims echoing the sphere in the second row of such a quilt.

Blocks Set On Point Without Sashing:
Quilt Set Model 8
We use the term "set on point" for blocks set in diagonal rows. We can describe the direction of these rows as running from lower left to upper right (or vice versa). For some reason, the diagonal set seems rare in the classic Album Quilts. Perhaps this is because so many of the block patterns have a top and bottom to them (bouquets, vases, buildings, lyres, hearts, etc.). Because the style had strong group ties, most blocks may have been designed specifically to set square, the more common American quilt set. The horizontal block set definitely dominates the Baltimore-style Albums. The diagonal set is a beauty, though, so we've given it a bit more play here than it had some 150 years ago.

Perhaps even in individually-made quilts, a few blocks were already completed before real thought was given to the set. By then the designs were already sewn for an "on square" set. A diagonal set also poses the problem of what to do with the half- and quarter-blocks, needed to square-off the quilt at its sides. In many quilts these appear to be whole blocks cut in half or in quarters. (It's fun to see which blocks have been "cannibalized." In one Album, a sweet house block has been sawed in two, to appear fleetingly at opposite edges of the quilt. To my mind this is the quilt's most charming square. Apparently not so to the quilt's maker.)

But more often, these partial blocks in the Album seem designed specifically to fit the needs of the set. (See Photos 4-12 and 4-22 in *Volume II*.) There is a magnificent contemporary group quilt, "Classic Revival Album," set on point in *Volume III*. Because I led that group I know that the decision to make a diagonally set quilt was there from the beginning. Each of those partial blocks was seized upon as a prime opportunity to present yet another *scherenschnitte* pattern for our series.

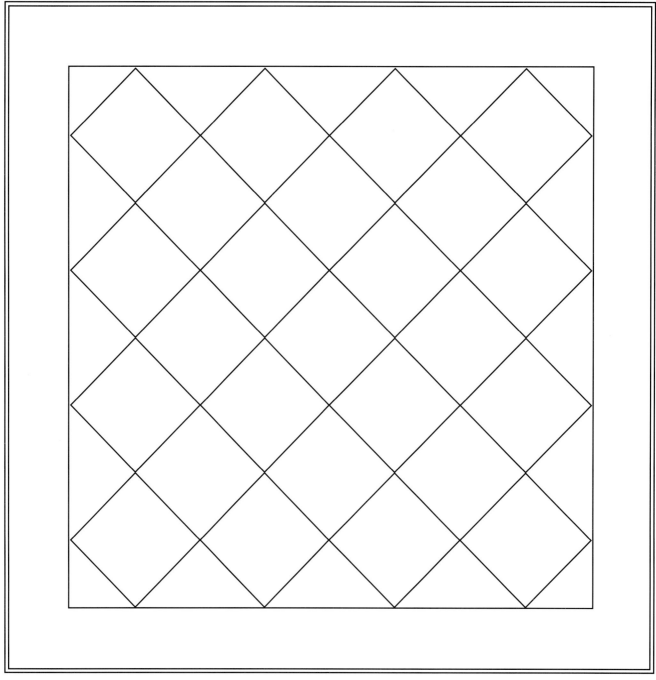

Quilt Set Model 8.
Twenty-five whole blocks (4 x 4) set on point without sashing and bordered.
The Gorsuch quilt (Photo 4-12, *Volume II*) admirably exemplifies this set.

Figure 2A-C.
Twenty-five block diagonal set, bordered.
These graphs are for Lesson 2's experiment with ways to emphasize the diagonal motion of this set. Three suggestions: Use A to
shade in a nine-block central medallion on point. Use B to shade
in the three whole blocks in each outer corner of the quilt. Use C
to shade in some internal pattern in the center nine-block medallion.

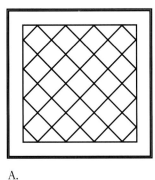
A.

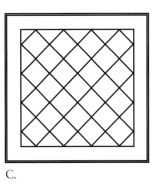
B.

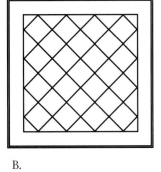
C.

Lesson 2: Poetry in Motion

Goal: To reinforce the concept of a diagonal line as
an exciting line in art because it conveys motion.
Vertical and horizontal lines are more static. Even in
a quilt set on point, you can do things to emphasize
this diagonal movement.

Exercise. Try to visually reinforce the diagonal
motion of this set. Use a pencil and simply shade in
(make more dense) selected squares on Figure 2. Do
you think any of the internal patterns suggested in
the caption were used in the vintage Gorsuch
Album (Quilt Set Model 8)? Can you suggest any
method the quiltmaker may have had in mind to
place those blocks as she did? The next section,
"Blocks and Medallions," will enumerate characteristics beyond density that make some blocks stand
out more than others. Perhaps these will help you
read that quiltmaker's mind more easily!

Figure 3A-B.
On-point sets for quilts with four or five whole blocks.
These graphs of two smaller on-point sets have no precedent in
the antique Albums that I know of. They are included here for
inspiration.

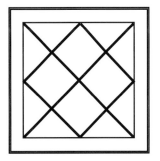

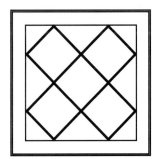

**A. Four whole blocks (2 x 2)
set on point with sashing and
bordered.**
This diagonal set has two
half-square triangles finishing
each corner. My impression is
that this set is very rare. I
have not seen this set as small
as 2 x 2, but it suits a modern
taste for smaller quilts. You
can see it in a much larger
quilt in Photo 4-22, *Volume
II.*

**B. Five whole blocks (2 x 2)
set on point with sashing and
bordered.**
This particular set squares the
quilt off with a one-quarter-
square triangle in its four
outer corners. It is seemingly
less rare in American quilts
than the previous type of set.
Again, I have not seen this set
as small as 2 x 2, but you can
visualize its potential beauty
by looking at a five-block
portion of the Follett House
Museum quilt pictured in
Quilt #7 in *Volume II.*

Blocks Set On Point with Sashing:
Quilt Set Models 9 and 10
My sense is that when blocks are diagonally set it was more often with sashing than without. Perhaps this is because the quiltmaker, in taking on the diagonal set, is already predisposed to take on even more work and complexity?

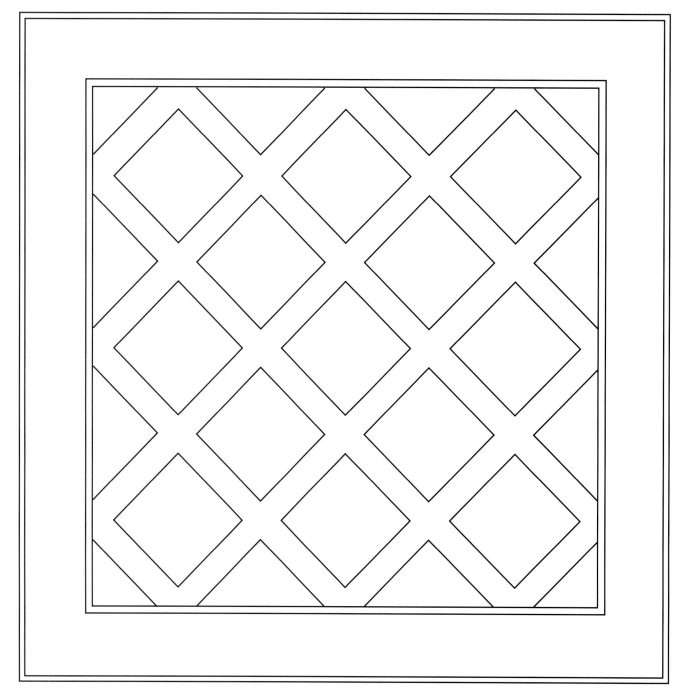

Quilt Set Model 9.
Thirteen whole blocks (3 x 3) set on point with sashing and bordered.
A perfectly exquisite version of this set is Quilt #7 in *Volume II*. The border here is slightly more than half the size of the block; the sashing is slightly less than one-third the size of the block.

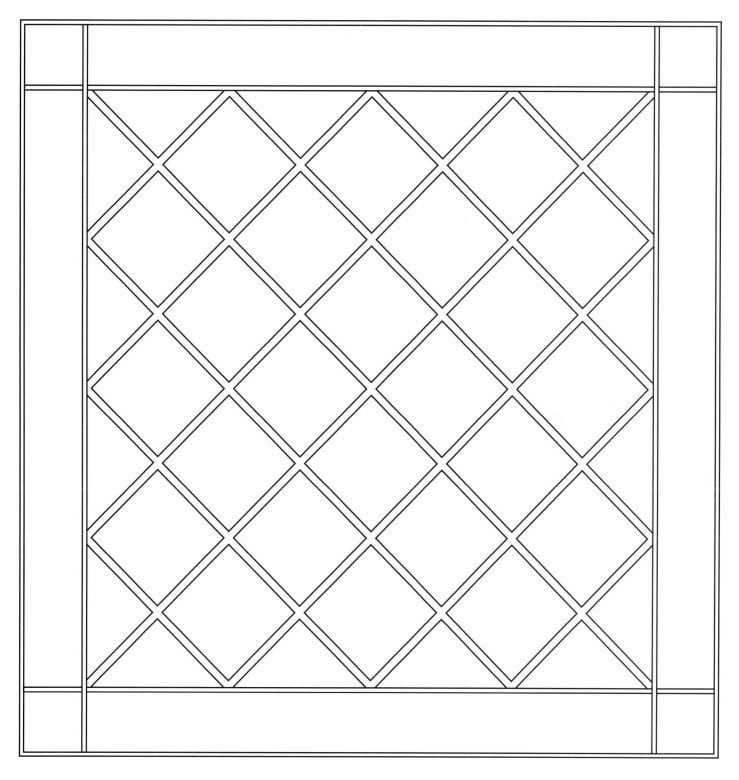

Quilt Set Model 10.

Twenty-four blocks (3 x 3) set on point with sashing and bordered. For an intriguing version of this rare set, see Photo 4-22 in *Volume II.* Chains (links of friendship and brotherhood) were a common motif in these quilts. Here they decorate the sashing. The border, however, is unusual. The same appliquéd chain motif defines all sides of each border as well as the border corners which have been left blank. The discrete and repeated fern frond unit suggests a wonderfully easy approach to an appliqué border. One could repeat any favored motif, evenly spaced, for this effect (see Figure 13D).

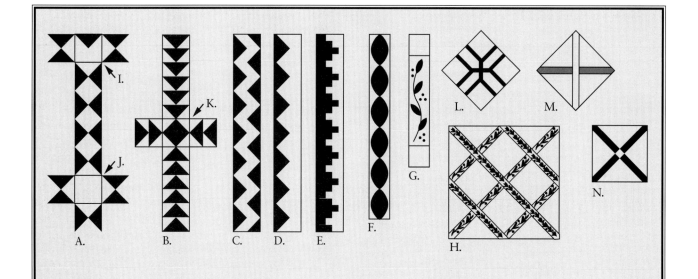

Picture This:

Sashings

Even after all these years, I am surprised at the elaborate conceptual detail in some of these antique quilts. Any given aspect (bindings, borders, baskets, even the phenomenal number of approaches to depicting roses) seems to have multiple levels of intricacy. Take the sashings, for example. These "block frames" cover a gamut of styles: wide or narrow, pieced or whole (print cloth or plain).

Sashings can be pieced in two or three pieced strips. They can be pieced of facing dogtooth triangles or diamonds (A), and pieced of "flying geese" triangles (B). Or they can be appliquéd with dogtooth triangles facing each other in a lightning streak set (C), or all in a row (D), with "steps" (E), chainlike elipses (F), or botanical themes (G). The greatest tour de force I've ever seen for appliquéd botanical sashings is the garlands of laurel sprigs (H) that twine between the 41 blocks in the 1844 Seidenstricker family Album. Look for these and more in the spectrum of classic Album Quilts. Note: Most often, the geometric sashings (triangles, steps) are red and white, occasionally green and white.

In the step and lightning streak sashings, the sashings run the full length of the blocks from top to botton, and are segmented (as though running underneath the full strips) as they run from left to right. In the laurel garland sashing, the whole garlands run on the diagonal, from upper left to lower right. Those they pass over are segmented. In none of these three sashings are corner blocks used.

Once one sashays down the sashing road, you come to the corners. We've all noted with delight those quilts where hearts (I) formed as the dogtooth triangle sashings intersect the outside sashings. In pleasing contrast, these same sashings form

diamonds (J) where they cross each other. A slightly different diamond (K) might bridge the crossed trails of flying geese. The "Garden Maze" set, too, has a beloved tradition of graphic paths and corner blocks (L). By far the most common sashings, though, are the simpler ones cut of one piece of fabric. Baltimore choices here were to make the vertical sashings appear as one piece, with the horizontals running "behind them" (M) or to use corner squares between the sashings (N).

Ponder this:

You are in charge of a pre-designed group quilt where each appliquéd block is to be turned in with two appliquéd sashings already sewn to it. Which two sashings (of those adjacent to every block) should these be? Phrase this assignment precisely so there will be no confusion in the quiltmaker's mind (and so the quilt sets together without a hitch!). More to think on: Can you slip into the Victorian mode and indulge in complex corners, at least on paper? What sort of sashing strip corners can you come up with? A flower-sprigged appliqué corner block (or certainly a heart) would be quicker and easier than appliquéd sashings. The concept may be a useful one. On a simple four-block wall quilt, for example, richness in sashings and/or corner blocks, combined with a substantial border, could make quite an elegant quilt. Use graph paper to help your thinking along.

II. Blocks and Medallions

Let's look at the nature of the block arrangements, themselves. The exercises start us off easily, using just small charts to represent the sets and penciled symbols to represent the design variable of different block pattern shapes. One of the most exciting concepts here is that the appliqué designs on the blocks themselves can set up internal patterns within the quilts. Excellent examples of this are in Figures 5 and 6. But first, let's get to know a bit more about all the block variables.

All blocks are not created equal. Your job is to play their differences to advantage and to make them work as an effective team. A block's power in the overall quilt set results from these variables: size of the block, shape of the block, density of the block's pattern, size and shape of its pattern, its location in the quilt (whether one of a kind or repeated, whether framed by sashing or not), distinctive color, and unexpected subject matter. These last two properties are especially familiar to most quiltmakers. For example, blocks with substantial amounts of "Baltimore Blue" would stand out in a predominantly red, white, and green quilt. Figurative blocks—a ship, a peacock, a person—catch the eye in a largely floral motif quilt.

These characteristics are among your tools in designing a quilt. Keep these variables in mind as you consider your block set. If the set you come up with looks ho-hum, try changing one (or more if necessary) of the variables. Let's look at them in a little more detail.

Most blocks are the same size in a Baltimore Album-style quilt. Sometimes, however, blocks are doubled to form rectangles, or quadrupled to form an enlarged medallion. Combined, they form an enlarged cross in the quilt's center. (See Figure 4B.) The arms of the cross are rectangles, the center is a large square, the corner blocks are smaller squares. Sometimes, as in Quilt #7 in *Volume I*, one block is repeated so that it reads as an enlarged medallion center. (See Figure 4C.) Blocks that are larger than those around them draw attention to themselves.

Density refers to how compact the appliqué pattern is. Dense blocks have relatively little white space showing within them. Blocks with appliqué patterns that appear "sparse" have more white space within the pattern. A sparse block surrounded by dense blocks stands out. Conversely, a dense block surrounded by sparse blocks stands out. So a block's power is relative to its position in the quilt. See this in the back cover quilt, the "Heart-Garlanded Album." Notice how carefully balanced the four corner quadrants of that quilt are.

Size affects a block's power. One can picture Albums with enlarged center blocks. In those cases, big is powerful. But the size of the appliqué's on same-size squares is also important. Consistency in size can help unify a quilt. If the size of the appliqués on our blocks differs substantially, we have three obvious choices: to arrange the diverse blocks in some sort of balance, or to unify the quilt with sashing running throughout, or to play up the size discrepancy (by location and/or repetition) to make a more dynamic quilt set.

What can lead to size discrepancy? It happens in a random collection of blocks whether by a group or individual. If patterns are all from one book or one designer, the blocks will tend to be consistent in size. Sometimes, however, a pattern initially drawn the same size as others finishes smaller. The appliqué shrinks (causing its background fabric rim to grow) in a pattern that involves an exceptional amount of stitching. Knowing this, you can take advantage of this size element. Theoretically, you could use repetitions of density, size, shape, or color to organize numbers of blocks into a design. But to me, the most exciting interior Album block patterns are created by repeated appliqué pattern shape.

These interior patterns are so distinct that you see them even in black-and-white illustrations. In fact, lack

Figure 4A-C. Block size and block shape.

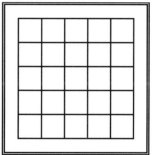

A. Most appliqué Albums have one consistent block size repeated throughout.

B. This is a classic block enlargement pattern. The doubled blocks form rectangles, the quadrupled blocks form an enlarged center medallion square.

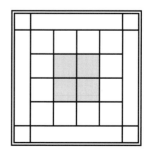

C. A peony block repeated four times and a simple strawberry block repeated four times form center blocks in antique Albums. Play with your block shapes and see what other blocks in multiple images might make dramatic medallion centers. Would any of them also look wonderful echoed in some way in the border or border corners?

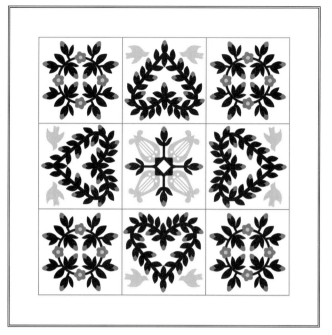

Figure 5.
"Mary's Garden" by Judy Severson. This quilt is on a hand-printed, embossed card from printmaker Judy Severson. Judy's use of interior pattern strikes me as brilliant. Can you see an eight-pointed star being formed by the white space here? In this "quilt," a slight modification in the two bottom flowers could close the points of the star.

Figure 6.
"Wedding Quilt" by Judy Severson. We learn another important lesson from this print: how identical blocks always read the same way. This symmetry seems important in establishing interior patterns. For purchase information on these cards, see Appendix II.

of color simplifies the lesson for us: white space in a block or quilt is negative space; black (or colored) space in a quilt is positive space. Both are powerful. We expect this power from the color. But, we may not have considered the effect the white space will have once our blocks are set together. The amount of white space around each appliquéd pattern affects the balance in a quilt set with sashing. But the real fun comes in when we use that white space as a repeated design element in a quilt. (See Figures 5 and 6.)

To use positive/negative space effectively, we need to analyze how different appliqué block shapes will read, and categorize them for design purposes. In the Block Gallery that follows, I've chosen certain representative shapes from my books and illustrated them with blocks.

Look at the Quilt Gallery in *Volume II*. See how open wreaths, for example, stand out. Squint at those black-and-white quilt photos and see if you would add shape categories of your own to my list. Perhaps you'll want to concentrate on the block style you like best and play with the patterns it creates when multiplied.

The Block Gallery:
Representative Pattern Shapes

These blocks are taken from my seven Album Quilt books. A pattern for each block here is given in the book noted. Multiples of these blocks are printed on the pull-out Pattern Resource Sheet. Cut up that sheet for your set model paste-ups. Then, if needed, you can photocopy more from these originals. The blocks are all 1" square to fit the set model. Use repositionable glue or tape so that you can rearrange the blocks easily. You can, of course, make your own representative block shapes: photocopy them out of the books and reduce them to the 1" square format.

In the Block Gallery, the shapes are arranged from lighter ones at the top of the page, to heavier blocks towards the bottom. Some blocks (square wreaths, for example) could be in multiple categories. I've placed each block in just one of its possible categories. Skim the following list of categories so that you'll be familiar with them as design tools when you do the lesson exercises.

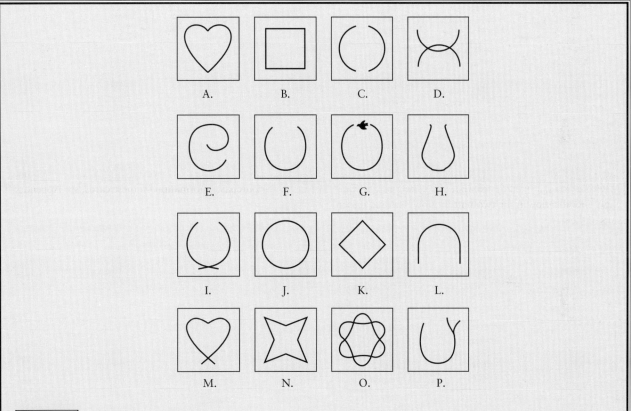

Picture this:

Open Wreaths: Geometry in Motion

A wreath is intertwined boughs, vines, or flower stems bound, usually into a circle. In geometry, we would describe the shape of a wreath as basically a drawn line. (The line follows the path of a point on one plane. In an Album block, that plane is the background fabric.) In the classic Album Quilts, wreath shapes (shown above) explore the possibilities of the drawn line.

Often breaks in the wreath-line are visually "closed" by a bird, butterfly, or bow. By and large, most of these "wreaths" can be made to read similarly in a quilt for purposes of orga-

nizing interior pattern. If you look at Quilt #9 in *Volume II*, you'll note that the main reason all the open wreaths read the same is that the blocks are all equally dense and the amount of white space is roughly the same in all. The ornate realistic wreaths tend to be dense, their shape echoed by interior white space that encloses a central (often asymmetrical) motif like a bird or bud. The term "open" refers to the white space within the wreath. Thus an open wreath reads quite differently than a dense circle or star shape. The consistency of effect (despite slight differences in the wreaths' shape) is part of what makes this quilt a masterpiece.

Key to the Block Gallery

A. **Blocks that read as Open Wreaths**
1. Crown of Laurel, Pattern #18, *Volume I*
2. Wreath of Cherries, Pattern #11, *Volume I*
3. Squared Grapevine Wreath, Pattern #10, *Volume II*
4. Broken Wreath of Roses, Pattern #19, *Volume I, Pattern Companion*
5. Bird in a Fruit Wreath, Pattern #13, *Volume II*
6. Roses for Hans Christian Andersen, Pattern #27, *Volume I, Pattern Companion*
7. Grapevine Wreath, Pattern in *Dimensional Appliqué*
8. Wreath and Dove, Pattern #25, *Volume I*

B. **Blocks that read as Lyre or Heart Wreaths**
1. Sweetheart Rose Lyre, Pattern #15, *Volume I*
2. Ruched Rose Lyre, Pattern #24, *Volume I*
3. Grapevine Lyre Wreath, Pattern #28, *Volume I, Pattern Companion*
4. Love, Pattern #13, *Volume I*
5. Hearts and Hands in a Feather Wreath, Pattern #9, *Volume II*
6. Feather-Wreathed Heart, Pattern #14, *Volume I*
7. Cherry Wreath with Bluebirds (I and II), Pattern #31, *Volume I, Pattern Companion*
8. Wreath of Hearts (I and II), Pattern #19, *Volume I*

C. **Blocks that read as Crossed Sprays or Crossed Diagonals**
1. Crossed Sprays of Flowers, Pattern #26, *Volume I, Pattern Companion*
2. Asymmetrical Spray of Red Blossoms I, Pattern #37, *Volume I, Pattern Companion*
3. Crossed Laurel Sprays, Pattern #7, *Volume I*
4. $200,000 Tulips, Pattern #8, *Volume I*
5. Fleur-De-Lis II, Pattern #2, *Volume I, Pattern Companion*
6. Crossed Pine Cones and Rosebuds, Pattern #3, *Volume II*
7. Victorian Favorite, Pattern #11, *Volume I, Pattern Companion*
8. Hospitality, Pattern #9, *Volume I*

D. **Blocks that read basically as Squares**
1. Fleur-de-Lis Medallion II, Pattern #21, *Volume I, Pattern Companion*
2. Fleur-de-Lis with Rosebuds III, Pattern #13, *Volume I, Pattern Companion*
3. Fleur-de-Lis and Rosebuds, Pattern page 21, *Spoken Without a Word*
4. Numsen Family Lyre, Pattern #11, *Volume II*
5. Joy Nichol's Rose of Sharon, Pattern #4, *Volume II*
6. Goose Girl Milking, Pattern #8, *Volume II*
7. Goose Girl, Pattern #15, *Volume II*
8. Acorn and Oak Leaf Frame, Pattern #6, *Volume II*

E. **Blocks that read basically as Diagonals**
1. Diagonal Floral Spray I, Pattern #32, *Volume I, Pattern Companion*
2. Diagonal Bough of Apples, Pattern #33, *Volume I, Pattern Companion*
3. Cherry Wreath with Bluebirds I and II, Pattern #31, *Volume I, Pattern Companion*
4. Bird Bedecked Bouquet, Pattern #35, *Volume I, Pattern Companion*
5. Cornucopia with Fruits and Acorns, Pattern page 61, *Spoken Without a Word*
6. Folk Art Vase of Flowers, Pattern #34, *Volume I, Pattern Companion*
7. Cornucopia from St. Louis Art Museum Album (pictured in Quilt #4, *Volume I, Pattern Companion*; pattern in *Volume III*)
8. Albertine's Rose Climber, Pattern #39, *Volume I, Pattern Companion*

F. **Blocks that read as Verticals**
1. Rose Lyre II, Pattern #22, *Volume I, Pattern Companion*
2. Flower Basket with Acorns, Pattern page 55, *Spoken Without a Word*
3. Bouquet avec Trois Oiseaux, Pattern #47, *Volume I, Pattern Companion*
4. Victorian Vase of Flowers III, Pattern #36, *Volume I, Pattern Companion*
5. Victorian Basket of Flowers IV, Pattern #41, *Volume I, Pattern Companion*
6. Vase of Roses I, Pattern #20, *Volume I*
7. A Token of Gratitude, Pattern #17, *Volume I*
8. Scalloped Epergne of Fruit, Pattern #44, *Volume I, Pattern Companion*

The Block Gallery
Representative Pattern Shapes

1.

2.

3.

4.

5.

6.

7.

8.

A. Open Wreaths B. Lyre or Heart Wreaths C. Crossed Sprays or Crossed Diagonals D. Squares E. Diagonals F. Verticals

Picture this:

Contemplating Symmetry

A certain "balanced asymmetry" characterizes the classic Baltimore-style Albums. When we concentrate for a minute on symmetry, we can see that the Album Quilts, for all their extravagant variety, really follow quite a controlled aesthetic. Both their blocks and their sets are rather tightly confined by parameters we recognize as "traditional." Quiltmaking within such carefully circumscribed principles of design almost reminds one of the fraternal injunction to "stay within compass." An antique engraving (see *Volume III*) of a young lady standing metaphorically within a circle advises, "Stay within compass, and you will be sure, to avoid many troubles, which others endure." The wisdom of balance in life as well as design is a core theme of Western Civilization. From classical Greece, Theognis's words "Moderation is best in all things" echo through the centuries to our space age ears. Our Victorian quiltmakers reflect Greek Revival ideals both of symmetry (epitomized by classic architecture) and balanced asymmetry (unrivaled in classic sculpture). Consider these aspects of symmetry:

I. Symmetrical Shapes (Being symmetrical, these are not directional. Therefore, they should be easy to balance in a quilt set.)
- A. Circles (symmetrical around a point)
- B. Eight-pointed stars (symmetrical on both sides of four axes)
- C. Squares (symmetrical on both sides of two axes)

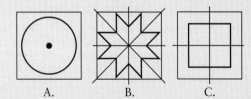

A.   B.   C.

II. Bisymmetrical Shapes (Bisymmetrical shapes are symmetrical along one axis. Thus they have direction. So bisymmetrical blocks can lead the eye in a certain direction within the quilt set. This is particularly true when the bisymmetrical shape is intentionally repeated in the quilt.)
- D. Diagonal sprays or baskets of fruit or flowers (symmetrical along one diagonal axis)
- E. Upright heart wreaths (symmetrical along a vertical axis) or trees or bushes

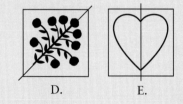

D.   E.

III. Asymmetrical Shapes (Asymmetrical shapes differ from one side of the axis or point to the other. Asymmetrical shapes can be repeated, thereby setting up secondary symmetrical patterns of their own.)
- F. Symmetrical around a point (A simple test of symmetry: When you cut through the center point of a symmetrical design, that cut line will always be equal on both sides of the point.)
- G. Asymmetrical around a point

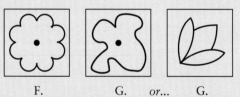

F.   G. *or...* G.

	SYMMETRY	ASYMMETRY
COLOR can be	symmetrical or	asymmetrical
SHAPE can be	symmetrical or	asymmetrical
DENSITY can be	symmetrical or	asymmetrical
SIZE can be	symmetrical or	asymmetrical

Symmetry can be around a horizontal axis, a vertical axis, a diagonal axis, or a point. When we contemplate the scope of symmetry and asymmetry, we can understand a bit better the depths of what feels like "traditional" to us in art. The folded paper-cut method (underlying so many of the one-, two-, and three-layer appliqué designs) by definition produces symmetry. To alter the symmetry of paper-cut designs takes intent, but we see it occasionally in the Album blocks. Keeping that asymmetry "in balance" takes, I think, some genius. One can appreciate the complexity of the Baltimore aesthetic when we look at the complicated asymmetrical, yet balanced, placement of the different blocks in "The Heart-Garlanded Album" diagrammed in Figure 8. Perhaps the maker charted her blocks out first to get a handle on the set!

Lesson 3: Tic Tac Toe

Goal: To see individual block patterns as simple shapes, themselves building blocks in an overall quilt design.

Exercise A. Using X's to represent crossed spray patterns and O's to represent wreath patterns, design a pleasing 25-block set. Fill it in with pencil on Figure 7B. See Figure 7A for samples.

Exercise B. Pencil the outline of a square to represent patterns which pretty much fill the block. Combine these squares with X's or O's (or both) and try to work out an interesting center focus to a 25-block quilt on Figure 7C.

Exercise C. Use what you learned from Exercise A or B to design a diagonally set quilt (13 or 41 blocks) with X's, O's, or squares. Or try any combination of two of those shapes. Use Figure 7D-E.

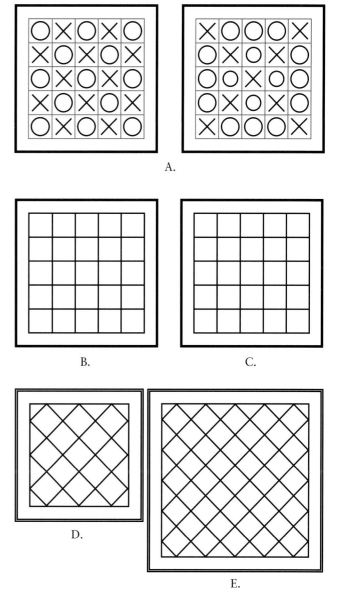

Figure 7.
Tic Tac Toe. Use these quilt diagrams to do Lesson 3.

Looking Ahead
In the next lessons we apply what we've learned from penciling in the symbols by arranging pictured block shapes. Then we want to isolate the steps of quilt design and to tackle one step at a time. We'll work the next exercises all the way through without getting involved in the border. While Albums were made both with and without borders, assume that these first "quilts" have background colored borders. Note: Pick and choose the lessons and the exercises that seem appealing. By simply reading over those that follow, you'll tuck them away as a seed planted for possible future use. Groups or classes working together may want to divide up the lessons to be done by "teams" who can share their results. If your assignment is to do just one exercise, you may want to go to the head of the class by making a paper and fabric mock-up of it!

Lesson 4: An Affair of the Heart

Goal: To create a recognizable shape (or interior design) of quilt blocks within a quilt using a heart-shaped wreath. See Figure 8 for samples done in symbols. Then do the exercises with actual blocks cut from the Pattern Resource Sheet.

Exercise A. Use one heart wreath, repeated, in a nine-block quilt to form some kind of interior pattern.

Exercise B. Repeat the same heart wreath shape in a twenty-five-block quilt to form an interior pattern. These can all be the same heart wreath pattern. Or you can use two or more different heart wreath patterns mixed.

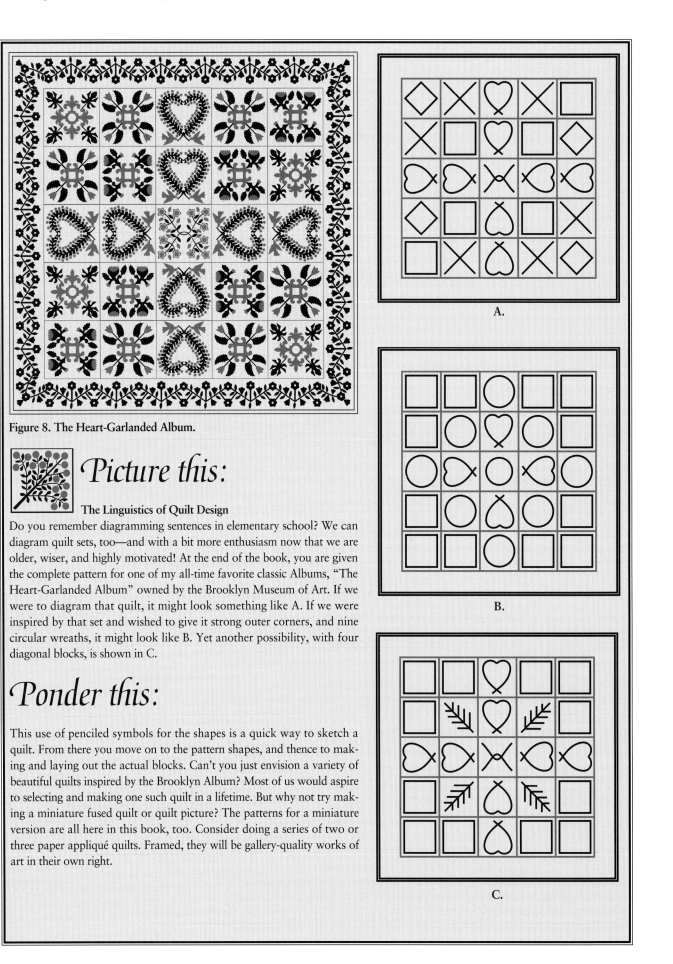

Figure 8. The Heart-Garlanded Album.

A.

B.

C.

Picture this:

The Linguistics of Quilt Design

Do you remember diagramming sentences in elementary school? We can diagram quilt sets, too—and with a bit more enthusiasm now that we are older, wiser, and highly motivated! At the end of the book, you are given the complete pattern for one of my all-time favorite classic Albums, "The Heart-Garlanded Album" owned by the Brooklyn Museum of Art. If we were to diagram that quilt, it might look something like A. If we were inspired by that set and wished to give it strong outer corners, and nine circular wreaths, it might look like B. Yet another possibility, with four diagonal blocks, is shown in C.

Ponder this:

This use of penciled symbols for the shapes is a quick way to sketch a quilt. From there you move on to the pattern shapes, and thence to making and laying out the actual blocks. Can't you just envision a variety of beautiful quilts inspired by the Brooklyn Album? Most of us would aspire to selecting and making one such quilt in a lifetime. But why not try making a miniature fused quilt or quilt picture? The patterns for a miniature version are all here in this book, too. Consider doing a series of two or three paper appliqué quilts. Framed, they will be gallery-quality works of art in their own right.

Lesson 5: Balanced, but Not Boring

Goal: To design a four-block quilt set that is pleasingly balanced, and has cohesion to the design. Do each exercise first on a horizontal set with no sashing. (Note: Four blocks present a challenge. It seems almost easier to frame, border, and build up one block into a small Album Quilt than to design four blocks into an exceptional Album Quilt. Using nine blocks becomes easy again, because you have a natural center focus and more blocks with which to build an interesting design.)

Exercise A. Repeat the same block shape (using the same or different patterns within that style) four times.

Exercise B. Repeat two different block shapes. Two out of four of the blocks should be directional (that is, vertical or diagonal).

Exercise C. Make a four-block quilt set using all different blocks.

Exercise D. You may feel that a four-block quilt needs something more. The border could certainly be the element that makes the difference. So could the sashing—or both. Which of the preceding four-block sets appeals to you as is? Set one of the preceding four-block arrangements with sashing. Does it appeal to you more or less this way? Set another one with four (or five) blocks on the diagonal. Does it appeal more or less this way?

Lesson 6: Good Fences Make Good Neighbors

Goal: To see if it is any easier to unify a diverse selection of blocks with the use of sashing or without.

Exercise A. Pick at least six block patterns, all different, and arrange them as best you can in a horizontal nine-block set without sashing.

Exercise B. Pick at least six different block patterns and arrange them as best you can in a horizontal nine-block set with sashing.

Exercise C. If it intrigues you, try this design problem on a larger quilt, with more blocks in greater diversity, but allow yourself to repeat some if the set calls for it. Consider that if the actual quilt is large, the sashing should probably be relatively narrow (1" to 1½") to separate, but not overwhelm the blocks.

Lesson 7: Ring Around the Rosey

Goal: To affect the central focus of the quilt by your choice of the corner blocks that ring the center.

Exercise. In a 25-block set, repeat the three blocks that form each corner. Try to choose blocks for both these corners and for the center that will result in a square on-point medallion formed by the different (non-corner) blocks.

Lesson 8: A Tisket, A Tasket

Goal: To repeat directional blocks in a set. Basket blocks are both charming and a challenge in a set because they have recognizable tops and bottoms to them.

Exercise A. Use four basket blocks in a nine-block set.

Exercise B. Use four or more vertical directional blocks (baskets, urns, vertical sprays, trees, or bushes) in a 25-block set.

Lesson 9: All Roads Lead to Rome (or "X Marks the Spot")

Goal: To focus on the central block in an odd-numbered set (9 or 25 same-sized blocks set square).

Exercise A. Try to create a diagonal crossroads (a strong visual line running on the diagonal from corner to corner) in the quilt by use of repeated blocks. What sort of blocks work well as an appropriate center? If no answer comes to mind, study pictures of the old quilts to see which center blocks work well.

Exercise B. Try to create a strong visual line that runs, centered, from the top border to the bottom border and perpendicular to both borders. Repeat this line between the side borders and have the two lines intersect in the middle.

Lesson 10: A Diamond Is a Girl's Best Friend

Goal: To explore the classic square-on-point medallion made of open wreaths.

Exercise. Try to echo the classic square-on-point medallion of eight open wreaths exemplified by the quilt in Photo 1. But this time, see if you can make the diamond work as effectively, using a block pattern shape other than a wreath.

Lesson 11: Using What You've Got

Goal: To become familiar with your own preferences in block placement. Often we know what we like, but haven't really thought about why we like it.

Exercise. Pick out 16 blocks randomly (even blindfolded) from your cut-apart pattern shapes. Imagine you have been given this quite magnificent gift of blocks and need to set them into a quilt. Put aside the issue of sashing and borders for the moment and just arrange the blocks. Make a list of the looks you like. For example, heavier blocks on the bottom just seem to appeal to me personally. If the quilt does not yet make one beautiful whole, move on to sashings and borders.

If you simply don't think that the quilt you've laid out is worthy of the blocks, you may do what I did with the original seven winners of the *Spoken Without a Word* block contest. I used those seven winners as the basis for three quilts (a 25-block, a 16-block, and a 9-block quilt), each of which has a quite different feeling to it. You will have learned something, though, by trying to arrange what you've got into a 16-block quilt. The more we concentrate, study, design and make quilts, the more likely our quilts are to sing with our very own muse's song.

The Medallion Gallery

"Medallion" refers to something the shape of a medal, usually a large oval or circle. In quilt parlance, though, a medallion has come to mean an enlarged center. The background fabric shape is an enlarged square or rectangle. The appliqué usually takes the form of a rounded square or circle. Medallion centers are out of the ordinary, something found in fancywork quilts. The next few lessons deal with medallions; five medallions whose patterns are in my books are shown here in the Medallion Gallery.

The Medallion Gallery

A. *Bowl of Flowers in a Rose Wreath.* (See Quilt #1 in the Color Section.) A pattern for both this medallion center and its accompanying border are in *Volume III.*

B. *Inscribed Wreath of Roses.* The color photograph, plus the complete pattern for both this medallion center and its accompanying border, are in *Dimensional Appliqué.*

C. *Feather-Wreathed Album in a Rose Lyre.* This is a variation of the Updegraf Album (Quilt #8 in *Volume II*) medallion center. It is shown in color in a glorious contemporary Album medallion in *Volume III.*

D. *Peony Medallion Center.* The four-block repeat center is a design concept that occurs more than once in mid-nineteenth-century Albums. See Quilts #7 and 8 in *Volume I.* The pattern is #38 in *Volume I, Pattern Companion.*

E. *Basket, Bird, and Book Medallion.* This is probably the most famous Baltimore Album Quilt center medallion. The complete pattern for the basket center and surrounding garland is in *Spoken Without a Word.* Another option is to use the shape of the garland, but fill it with your own foliage, fruits, or flowers. It could also surround a picture block of a house or monument.

Figure 9A-E.
Medallions are enlarged center blocks. The most powerful characteristic of medallions is their multiple block size. Each of the medallions pictured here follows the 1" block scale needed to paste them into your block set diagrams.

Lesson 12: Multiples

Goal: To design your own repeat block medallion center.

Exercise A. Choose a simple symmetrical block and repeat it four times. Play with block picture cut-outs from the Pattern Resource Sheet. What set of blocks works as a repeat block center? Consider the direction(s) in which the block will sit.

Exercise B. Design a repeat block medallion center using an asymmetrical block. Choose a simple asymmetrical block and repeat it four times. How does this compare with the symmetrical repeat block center? Which pleases you more? Consider the direction(s) in which the block will sit.

Lesson 13: We're All in This Together

Goal: To vary a medallion center of four repeated blocks so that the design links the blocks together visually to form a center medallion.

Exercise. Consider whether you might want to, somehow, link your choice of repeated center blocks. For example, the heart at the center of the Odense Album border (Border Gallery: III. #10) is an integral part, almost a knot, in the vine border. Could you link four hearts together as a center medallion? Do you think it might be easier to link symmetrical blocks than asymmetrical blocks? Can you design some sort of wreath-shape block (a heart or other wreath) that lends itself more easily to being linked, one to the other?

Lesson 14: It's a Frameup!

Goal: To design a frame for an enlarged (four-block size) center medallion. Medallions seem full of unprobed potential. A quilt I would love to see would have a laurel wreath framing a national monument like the U.S. Capitol (or a cherry blossom wreath garlanding the Jefferson Monument).

Exercise A. Design an enlarged block frame formed by a wreath. For a basic shape and placement diagram, you could use the Central Medallion garland from *Spoken Without a Word* or the Ringgold Album Medallion (Quilt #1 in the Color Section). Or, you could simply sketch one-quarter of the enlarged frame by marking an arc on a 12½" square of paper (anchor the compass at the lower right-hand block corner). Consider four garland arcs (one on each of the squares that make up the center medallion) joined by tied ribbon bows. Even an elegant inscription traced in bold calligraphy inside the wreath would be a dramatic quilt center.

Exercise B. Design a papercut frame (such as those used for picture blocks in *Volume II*) for a sixteen-block quilt. Approach: design on a 12½" square of paper, folding it into eighths as directed in *Volume II*. If you make a design with potential, have one-eighth of it enlarged photographically at the printer to a four-block size. Use this as the master template to cut a full-sized pattern. The truly exciting thing, to me, about medallion frames, is that you can set a normal-sized block (a basket, for example) inside the frame. The key fact is the center of the four-square-sized medallion frame should line up exactly with the center of your 12½" appliquéd block. It can be a block that you have already made and want to stage dramatically. And if you have successfully designed a papercut medallion frame, by all means accept the invitation to go on and design a papercut border!

III. Borders

Not all Baltimore-style Albums had borders. But to make an outstanding appliqué Album without a border is to accomplish what the classic set reproduced in Photo 1 does. There the quilt is self-bordered by the size and placement of its blocks. The simplest of borders can make a masterful quilt. The DAR Museum's quilt in Photo 4-8 in *Volume II* has a plain white (beautifully quilted) border. That border seems to make all the difference in that quilt. Another, even simpler border is the green calico one in Photo 4-10 in the same volume. The simplest one-layer border can be elaborate when made of an elegant print as in Photo 4-34 in *Volume II*. The second simplest kind of border is the pieced border (strips, saw-tooth, or flying geese triangles). Can you find picture examples of these?

Take a minute to flip through your Album Quilt books and fill your mind with all the borders that adorn these quilts. Watch for the details in these borders: Where and in what various ways do borders start and stop? Would it be easier to size a broken border than a continuous one? Can you find quilts where there is more than one border used, either concentrically or on different sides of the quilt? Do you see quilts whose corners differ substantially from the running border motif? Can you find corners that differ from each other? My experience has been that these very complex quilts need either to be self-bordered or to be framed by a separate border to present them well.

This border section includes fundamental techniques for both sizing a given pattern to your quilt set and for designing running or repeated discrete motif borders of your own. Any border your heart desires should be at your fingertips! The Gallery Tour in *Volume II* discussed borders thoroughly. Let's review them here in the lessons and in the Border Gallery.

The Border Gallery

Appliquéd Edging Borders

Edging borders frame the border. They usually have a solid base of 1/2" or so, leading to the appliquéd design that faces in towards the center of the border. This center may have no appliqué, but rather a running vine or feather plume may be quilted into its white space. Or it can have an appliqué design such as a center-running vine. Sometimes an edging appliqué is done on either the inside or the outside of the border, sometimes on both sides. Familiar edging borders from appliqué Albums are dogtooth triangles, steps (two, three, and six steps), scallops or ruffles, or cutaway appliqué motifs like the Peony Border or the Canopy of Heaven Border.

Appliquéd Running Borders

A running border is a colloquial term for a motif that is joined (or, at least, the design does not dramatically break) across the length of a border. Common motifs are hammocks or swags (joined by flowers, ribbons, stars, etc.), leafed vines (often with fruit and/or flowers), and feather plumes (often reverse appliquéd from white to red). There are also borders made of discrete motifs such as leaves or flowers, or flowers and birds. These can be placed with their axis vertical or horizontal. They, too, "run" across the border in their repetitions, but we see them more as separate motifs.

These quilt borders are drawn out both as full frames (so that you can see their layout) and printed in strips for design paste-up. For your convenience, the pull-out Pattern Resource Sheet shows the border strips as well as the representative block shapes. Every border shown has a full-scale pattern in the *Baltimore Beauty* series. The borders in the Border Gallery are keyed to the list below; Roman numerals indicate the book in which the borders *originally* appear (or in the case of *Dimensional Appliqué* and *Volume III*, will appear). For example, in the Border Gallery, "III.#1. Grapevine Border" indicates that the Grapevine Border originally appeared in *Baltimore Beauties and Beyond, Volume II*.

I.   *Baltimore Beauties and Beyond, Volume I*
II. *Baltimore Album Quilts, Volume I, Pattern Companion*
III. *Baltimore Beauties and Beyond, Volume II*
IV. *Design a Baltimore Album Quilt!*
V.   *Dimensional Appliqué—Baskets, Blooms, and Baltimore Borders*
VI. *Baltimore Beauties and Beyond, Volume III*

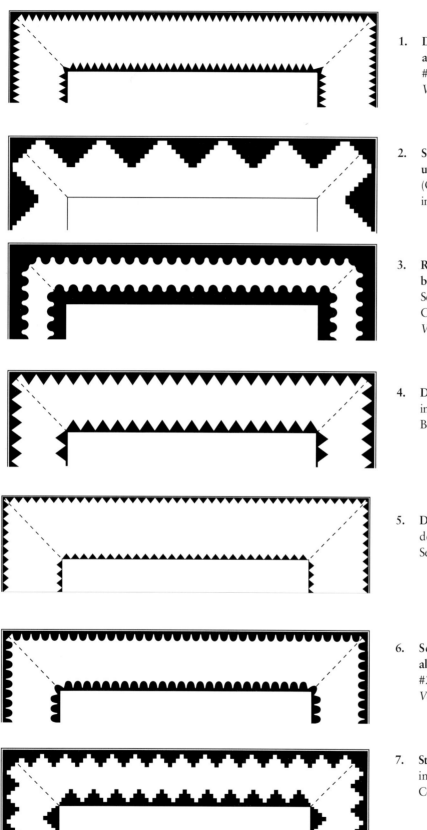

1.   **Dogtooth Border (of a size to be used alone).** See this border in *Volume II* (Quilt #11 in the Color Section). Pattern #26 in *Volume II*.

2.   **Stepped Border (six steps, of a size to be used alone).** See this border in *Volume II* (Quilt #6 in the Color Section). Pattern #27 in *Volume II*.

3.   **Ruffled Border (of a size used as an edging border with a center-running vine border).** See this border in *Volume I* (Quilt #2 in the Color Section). Border pattern #28 in *Volume II*.

4.   **Dogtooth Triangle Border I.** See this border in *Volume I* (Quilt #6 in the Color Section). Border pattern #29 in *Volume II*.

5.   **Dogtooth Triangle Border II.** See this border in *Volume I* (Quilt #7 in the Color Section). Border pattern #30 in *Volume II*.

6.   **Scalloped Border (of a size to be used alone).** See this border in *Volume II* (Quilt #2 in the Color Section). Pattern #31 in *Volume II*.

7.   **Stepped Border (three steps).** See this border in *Volume II* (Quilts #4 and #17 in the Color Section). Pattern #32 in *Volume II*.

I. #1. Angular Rose Vine Border from Quilt #2, Classic Baltimore Album Quilt. Pattern in *Dimensional Appliqué*.

I. #2. Hammock and Bow Border from Quilt #6, The Good Ladies of Baltimore. Pattern in *Volume II*.

I. #3. Peony and Hammock Border from Quilt #7, The Fascinating Ladies of Bygone Baltimore. Pattern in *Volume II*.

I. #4. Friendship's Offering Border from Quilt #8, Friendship's Offering. Pattern in *Volume III*.

I. #1. I. #2. I. #3. I. #4.

II. #1.   III. #1.   III. #2.   III. #3.

III. #1.Grapevine Border from Quilt #1, Appliquéd Medallion Quilt. Pattern in *Dimensional Appliqué*.

III. #2. Scalloped Edging Border from Quilt #2, Classic Baltimore Album Quilt. Pattern #24 in *Volume II*.

II. #1. Mrs. Mann's Quilt Border from Quilt #3, Classic Baltimore Album Quilt. Pattern in *Dimensional Appliqué*.

III. #3. Rosebud Border from Quilt #4, Classic Baltimore Album Quilt. Pattern in *Dimensional Appliqué*.

III. #4. Solid Striped Border from Quilt #5, Classic Baltimore Album Quilt. No pattern given.

III. #5. Six-step Edging Border from Quilt #6, Classic Baltimore Album Quilt. Pattern #27 in *Volume II*.

III. #4.   III. #5.   III. #6.   III. #7.

III. #6. Beribboned Feather Border from Quilt #8, Classic Baltimore Album Quilt. Pattern in *Volume III*.

III. #7. Printed striped border from Quilt #10, Baltimore-style Album Quilt. No pattern given.

III. #8.   III. #9.   III. #10.   III. #11.

III. #9. Peony Border from Quilt #13, More Maryland Flowers. Pattern #21 in *Volume II.*

III. #10. Dancing Grapevine Border from Quilt #17, the Odense Album. Pattern in *Dimensional Appliqué.*

III. #8. Triangle Edging Border (with vine-quilted space in between) from Quilt #11, Classic Baltimore Album Quilt. Pattern #26 in *Volume II.*

III. #11. Canopy of Heaven Border. See Photo 4-4 and Pattern #33 in *Volume II.*

III. #12. Reverse Feather Plume Border from Classic Baltimore Album Quilt. See Photo 4-14 in *Volume II*. Pattern in *Design a Baltimore Album Quilt!*

IV. #1. Border from the Heart-Garlanded Album. Pattern in *Design a Baltimore Album Quilt!*

IV. #2. Border from the Sarah Shaefer Album on the front cover. Pattern in *Design a Baltimore Album Quilt!*

IV. #3. Laurel Leaf Border. Pattern in *Design a Baltimore Album Quilt!*

III. #12.   IV. #1.   IV. #2.   IV. #3.

IV. #4.

IV. #5.

V. #1.

V. #2.

IV. #5. Mirrored Ribbon Border from Quilt #2, Album Quilt, in the Color Section. Pattern in *Volume III*.

V. #1. Leafy Border from Baltimore-style Album Quilt. Pattern in *Dimensional Appliqué*.

IV. #4. Straight Rose Vine Border from Quilt #1, Classic Baltimore Album Quilt, in the Color Section. Pattern in *Volume III*.

V. #2. Rose of Sharon Border from Baltimore-style Album Quilt. Pattern in *Volume III*.

VI. #1. Palmetto-tied Laurel-Garlanded Border, from the Classic Revival Album. Pattern in *Volume III*.

VI. #2. Tassled Ribbon Swag Border from Baltimore-style Album Quilt. Pattern in *Volume III*.

VI. #3. Bonnie's Hearts and Angels Ruffled Swag Border by Kathryn Blomgren Campbell. Pattern in *Volume III*.

VI. #4. Homegrown Rose Border, from Baltimore-style Album Quilt. Pattern in *Volume III*.

VI. #1.   VI. #2.   VI. #3.   VI. #4.

Part Two continued on page 66

The Color Section

There are quilts whose image we hold in the mind's eye. At first forceful and immediate, their impression is also lasting. More intimate inspection rewards us with wondrous and endearing detail, just hinted at in the first glance. The detail confirms their appeal. But it was the presentation, that first overall impression, that enamored us and drew us closer.

Such quilts are rare, in my experience. And the flower-centered medallion quilt that opens our Color Section is surely one of them. Its presentation is dramatic. A handsome border (simple yet appropriate) enhances a fascinating array of blocks. The bright rose wreath border is echoed by the center medallion wreath. Within the medallion is a refreshingly graphic vase of flowers. It seems to be of the distinctive folk art Baltimore Album style that may reflect German origins.

This quilt's border and medallion, in concert, present an enviable collection of blocks. If, indeed, these Album Quilts were "collections on a theme," this collection seems almost complete. Unified by color palette, the diverse styles and themes are delightfully recognizable to the Album Quilt connoisseur: the heavily stuffed and embroidered style (attributed by Dr. William Rush Dunton to the German influence), the German folk art style, the Ringgold Mexican War Memorial, the picture blocks, the wreaths of apples and roses, the (cutaway appliqué) baskets of fruits and flowers, and the ornate, realistic Victorian-style blocks with their expressive fabrics, their layered look, and inked and embroidered embellishments. Most of the Albums' key themes are represented: the Rebekah dove and olive branch; the Odd Fellow cornucopias in links of red, yellow, and blue; fruits in epergnes, extolling the earth's bountiful blessings; and flowers in urns for the sweetness of the soul.

This Color Section presents three antique Album Quilts and thirty-eight contemporary Albums. The latter range from full-sized twenty-five-block Albums to one-block wall quilts, with nine- and sixteen-block quilts in between. Each shows its maker's particular joy in these Albums; each tells a story. Many have been made with a theme or a person in mind and are wonderfully evocative. All show remarkable artistry, creativity, and self-expression. Though ornate, complex, and diverse, the Victorian Album style has been learned so well that these quiltmakers have made it their own. With the confidence born from knowing one's medium thoroughly, several of these quilt artists have made unique, yet stylistically unified Albums. They have taken Baltimore substantively "beyond." It excites me that not only the aesthetics of Baltimore have been stretched exuberantly, but that this innovation has also focused on the conceptual framework of the Baltimore-style Albums. Albums such as Patricia L. Styring's (Quilt #4), Marian Brockschmidt's (Quilts #6 and #7) and June Dixon's (Quilt #8) express highly personalized themes in a closely held Baltimore style.

Equally self-expressive, but stretching the style even further, are Quilts #40 and #41. Katherine L. McKearn first made an exquisitely unique Baltimore-style Album, "The Baltimore County Album Quilt" (*Quilter's Newsletter Magazine*, May 1992). Reflecting its pastoral theme (Baltimore County as distinct from Baltimore City), gracefully portrayed fruit and vegetable still lifes surround the center medallion's book (a seed catalogue) and basket. Pushing the Album style even further, Ms. McKearn follows a Picasso-like progression. Like Picasso, her earlier work proves that she can do exceptional representational portrayal in the classic mode. Having made that classic mode her own, she (in "Allegheny Avenue Album," Quilt #40) gives her artistry, her imagination (even her wry humor), freer rein.

Marilyn Hamaker, too, first made a more traditional Album, then wove two Album threads (symbolic appliqué motifs and "collections on a theme") into a stitched paean to cinema's golden age (Quilt #41). Cleverly, she incorporated details reminiscent of the era into a quilt so astonishingly "beyond Baltimore" that its family ancestry is recognizable only to those who know and love those fascinating ladies well. You'll find more about these quilts and their makers in Part Four, "About the Needleartists." Now, let's enjoy the gallery of Albums presented here.

QUILT #1
Flower-centered Medallion Album Quilt.
Mid-nineteenth century. "Assembled and quilted by Sarah Anne
Whittington Lankford, b. 1830, d. 1898." 84" x 99".
Accession #79.609.14. *(Photo courtesy of Abby Aldrich*
Rockefeller Folk Art Center, Colonial Williamsburg, Virginia)

QUILT #2 *(Left)*
Album Quilt. American. Circa 1855. 83$^{1}/_{2}$" x 84$^{1}/_{2}$".
Gift of Miss Eliza Polhemus Cobb, through Mrs. Arthur
Bunker, 1952. Accession #52.103. *(Photo courtesy of the
Metropolitan Museum of Art)*

QUILT #3 *(Below)*
Album Quilt. American. "Baltimore. Maker: members of the
Brown and Turner families, begun in 1846. 83$^{3}/_{8}$" x 85".
All blocks are signed by different hands, some in ink, some in
cross stitch." Bequest of Margaret Brown Potvin, 1987.
Accession #1988.134. *(Photo courtesy of the Metropolitan
Museum of Art)*

DETAIL OF QUILT #4 *(Right)*
Original design by Patricia L. Styring, showing a skillful ease and delight in
making the ornate, realistic Victorian style of the classic Baltimore Albums her
very own.

QUILT #4 *(Below)*
Patricia L. Styring. "Baltimore Album Nouveau with Angels." 85" x 85".
Angels are rare in the Baltimore-style Albums, occuring in only one block that
I know of (see Photo 4-34 in *Baltimore Beauties and Beyond, Volume II*).
(Photo courtesy of American International Quilt Association)

QUILT #5 *(Left)*

Carol Spalding. "Floral Miniature." 1991. 30" x 30". This original design combines traditional appliqué, *Broderie Perse*, fabric painting, and embroidery to produce in miniature the effect of a full Baltimore Album Quilt. Note the diamond sashing corner blocks, a charmingly unique touch in this quilt's set. *(Photo courtesy of Sharon Risedorph)*

QUILT #6 *(Below)*

Marian Brockschmidt. "Martha's Baltimore and Beyond." 1991. 91" x 91". Marian made this lovely quilt for her eight-year-old granddaughter, Martha {"as a wedding present"}. A remarkable sampler of elegant Album blocks, Marian's set and border frame them to perfection. *(Photo courtesy of William Brockschmidt)*

QUILT #7 *(Right)*
Marian Brockschmidt. "Kevin and Jami's Wedding Baltimore and Beyond." 1992. 68" x 68". This Album, Marian's third, was made for her grandson's wedding. Kevin, a cartoonist and pilot, designed the picture block on the right. His wife, Jami, raised on a farm, is represented by the traditional "Goose Girl Milking" block on the left. Note how the strong sashing and appliquéd border here give added stature to the simplicity of a nine-block quilt. *(Photo courtesy of William Brockschmidt)*

QUILT #8 *(Below)*
June Dixon. "745th Tank Battalion Album Quilt." 1989-1991. 90" x 90". June mixed blocks of her own design with those from *Spoken Without a Word* and *Baltimore Beauties and Beyond*. Using both picture blocks and military symbols, June made this stately and handsome Album Quilt in honor of her husband's tank batallion (which served in the European theater in World War II) and all other U.S. veterans. *(Photo courtesy of Sharon Risedorph)*

QUILT #9 *(Right)*
Linda Halpin. "Appliqué à la Mode." 1987. 25" x 25". With a fascination for appliqué techniques and a flair for incorporating symbolism into the quilting design, Linda's choice of airy set and simple border for this miniature Album makes it a small gem. *(Photo courtesy of Tom Leininger)*

QUILT #10 *(Left)*
Marilyn Norris Hamaker. "Baltimore Sampler." 1990. 24" x 24". Marilyn adapted patterns from *Baltimore Beauties and Beyond (Volume I)* to a 6" format to "try out the various appliqué methods." Having re-drafted all the blocks and borders, and made them out of a limited fabric palette, Marilyn produced a quilt with a strong and pleasing individualism and style. *(Photo courtesy of Rob Goebel)*

QUILT #11 *(Right)*
Cheryl A. Spence. "Twenty-fifth Anniversary." 1990-1991. 56" x 56". "Four corner blocks refer to the four cities that we have lived in during 25 years of marriage—London, St. Louis, Washington, D.C., and Indianapolis. Center block refers to our marriage date, and top and bottom center blocks refer to the birth dates of our two sons." Cradling all that significance is a strikingly original and successful Album set and border. *(Photo courtesy of Rob Goebel)*

QUILT #12 *(Left)*
Dianne Miller. "Amour Galore." 1989-1992. 68" x 68".
This is Dianne's interpretation of classic Baltimore blocks using Christmas colors and her original border design. The quilt has a lovely cohesiveness and dynamism. The circular set "corners" add a joyful sparkle to the set. *(Photo courtesy of Paul Miller)*

QUILT #13 *(Right)*
 Judy Pleiss. "Memories of Love and Caraway Cookies." 1990-1991. 64" x 64". A quilt portrait of Judy's rural New Hampshire heritage, this depicts the people, places, and animals, as described by her mother in 1927. Her mother's writings are silk screened to the back of the quilt. Judy's charming design shows her sheer pleasure in the expressive potential of the Album genre. *(Photo courtesy of Rob Goebel)*

QUILT #14 *(Left)*
Anita Hardwick. "My Country Garden." 1990-1991.
87" x 87". The quilt was entirely designed by Anita including drafting the star and designing the original appliqué. It is a dramatically successful quilt created in the heirloom Album tradition. *(Photo courtesy of Rob Goebel)*

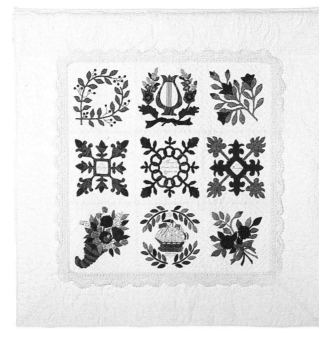

QUILT #15 *(Above)*
Eveline Howes. "Johannesburg and Beyond." 1990-1991.
38" x 38". "This quilt represents the story of our family first in
South Africa and then in the U.S. The handmade lace surrounding the blocks was in my mother's lace box for as long as I can
remember and this seemed the perfect place to preserve it." This
exquisite quilt eloquently confirms the power of a white border.
(Photo courtesy of Rob Goebel)

QUILT #16 *(Above)*
Alice Hyde. "Mother's Album Quilt." 1985-1989. 84" x 102".
"Mother's Album Quilt with eight wreath blocks signed by
children of Albert and Rachel Hyde surround a center cornucopia block." Alice's artistic use of the laurel spray borders top
and bottom not only make the quilt rectangular, but add to its
lightness and elegance as well. *(Photo courtesy of Bruce Belling)*

QUILT #17 *(Left)*
Betty Alderman. "Family Album." 1989-1992.
66 1/2" x 66 1/2". Betty's design motifs from
nineteenth-century quilts surround her wonderful
picture block portrait of the family home. The
relaxedly spaced set uses the white areas skillfully
and surrounds the quilt with a delightful border's
sampling of quilt motifs. Betty's original design, the
border echoes the freedom of those nineteenth-
century quilts where the pattern changes at the
maker's whim. *(Photo courtesy of Phil Pendleton)*

QUILT #18 *(Right)*
Ruth Meyers. "Hearts and Birds." 1991. Approximately
60" x 60". The intricacy of Ruth's appliquéd blocks are set off
spaciously and framed with restrained elegance by the striped
border of plain fabric bound by a sophisticated dark striped
print. *(Photo courtesy of Sharon Risedorph)*

QUILT #19 *(Left)*
Arnold Savage. "Baltimore-style Presentation Quilt Opus 50."
1990-1991. Machine appliqué. 75" x 87". Several blocks are
original designs by the maker, but, notes Mr. Savage, "Most of
them are based on research from all currently available books,
William Rush Dunton's *Old Quilts* being of great help."
(Photo courtesy of Arnold Savage)

QUILT #20 *(Right)*
The Good Ladies of Baltimore North and the Cocheco Quilters
Guild of Dover, New Hampshire (Faye Labanaris, coordinator).
Group quilt. "Baltimore Friends." 1988-1992. 80" x 80".
"This raffle quilt is composed of donated blocks from Baltimore
friends/students." The proportions of white space and the
chintz print choice for the diamonds and borders are felicitous.
(Photo courtesy of George Maccabee)

QUILT #21 *(Left)*
Lisa Byers. "Discovery Quilt 1492-1992." 1991-1992.
Approximately 77" x 77". The Ladies Auxiliary of
Water Mill created this raffle quilt, in honor of the
five-hundredth anniversary of Columbus's voyage, as a
fund-raiser for the Water Mill Museum in Water Mill,
New York. Original and traditional designs were used.
(Photo courtesy of Southampton Aeroservice, Inc.)

QUILT #22
Marlene Peterman. Bride's Quilt. "Love Conquers All."
1988. 100" x 108". " 'Love Conquers All' was inspired
by the Baltimore quilts of Pat Cox and Bernice Enyeart
and furthered by Elly." Sherbert colors and rectangular
insets with doves enhance the sheer prettiness of this
quilt. *(Photo courtesy of Jack Mathieson)*

QUILT #23
Baltimore Heritage Quilt Guild (Mimi Dietrich, coordinator).
"Baltimore Album Quilt." 1990. 96" x 96". This is a group raffle
quilt made by the 40 members of the Baltimore Heritage Quilt Guild.
The block patterns belong to *Woman's Day Magazine*; Robert Wilson
designed the border. The quilt took 18 months to complete. *(Photo
courtesy of the Baltimore Heritage Quilt Guild)*

QUILT #24 *(Right)*
Karen Brown Bludorn. "Dances with Flowers."
1990-1992. 82" x 92". "Used Elly's, Jeanna
Kimball's, Nancy Pearson's, and my own
original designs. The border is my design." And
the bed-tailored border is a charmer! *(Photo
courtesy of Karen Bludorn)*

QUILT #25 *(Below right)*
Mississippi Valley Quilters Guild (Maureen
Carlson, coordinator). "Wreaths, Roses, and
Ribbons." 1991-1992. 92"x 92". Raffle quilt
for the 1992 National Quilting Association show
in Davenport, Iowa. The patterns for the 16
blocks are from the *Baltimore Beauties* series; the
border is original. Made of 100% cotton hand
dyes, this is a "traditional design executed in a
nontraditional manner." *(Photo courtesy of Bob
French)*

DETAIL OF QUILT #25
Kim Churbuck. Quilt Label. 15" x 20".
This lovely label was inspired by the
quilt's design motifs. Sewn to the quilt's
back, it documents the project.

ONE-BLOCK QUILTS *(See captions on page 65)*

QUILT #26 *(Above left)*
Ellen Peters. "Grapevine Lyre."

QUILT #27 *(Above right)*
Marlene Peterman. "Appliqué an Heirloom."

QUILT #28 *(Left)*
Donna Bailey. "Sky Flowers."

QUILT #29 *(Below left)*
Ellen Peters. "Fleur-de-Lis."

QUILT #30 *(Below right)*
Claire Jarratt. "Friendship."

ONE-BLOCK QUILTS *(See captions on page 65)*

QUILT #31 *(Above)*
Marlene Peterman. "Spring Basket."

QUILT #32 *(Above right)*
Ellen Peters. "Sweetheart Rose Lyre."

QUILT #33 *(Right)*
Niki Baker. "Baltimore Bouquet."

QUILT #34 *(Below left)*
Ellen Peters. "Crown of Laurel."

QUILT #35 *(Below right)*
Ellen Peters. "Feather-Wreathed Heart."

QUILT #36 *(Left)*
Betsy Harris. "Delusions of Baltimore." 1990-1991.
48" x 48". This quilt's center block is a heartwarmingly original rendition of the quiltmaker's "loghouse and menagerie, including a hummingbird." This appealing quilt works surprisingly well unbordered. *(Photo courtesy of Rob Goebel)*

QUILT #37 *(Below)*
Dolores Smith Brock. "Baltimore Album—Yuma Style." 1987-1991. 75" x 75". The gay informality, here, of the beribboned medallion center echoes certain older Albums. "The bottom right-hand block is a personalized block," writes Dolores. "With me being born in Arkansas, I placed a rebel flag and a razorback hog in this, also my VW bug and other items." *(Photo courtesy of Alan Lochotzki)*

QUILT #38 *(Right)*
Ethel Howey. " 'Ai,' My Mother." 1992. 80" x 96".
Restraint and grace characterize this memorable Album. It
combines Japanese and American fabrics and motifs with the
ease of an artistic American quiltmaker born of Japanese
parents. Even the quilt's name "Ai," which means 'love,' has
woven meanings, since Ai is also the name of Ethel's mother
whom this quilt celebrates. The fan border is nothing less
than stunning. Wavelike, it imparts a contained (yet exciting)
motion, and a sculptural, three-dimensional quality to this
quilt built of the more one-dimensional paper-cut-appliqué-
style blocks. Even in those flat cut-outs, the differing intensi-
ties of hue in the prints evoke shifting layers of depth and
light. *(Photo courtesy of Sharon Risedorph)*

QUILT #39 *(Below)*
Shirley Tickle. "Grandeur." 1990-1991. 103" x 105".
This intricate and well-met challenge was Shirley's first
appliqué. The concept of elongated blocks is recurring, but
quite rare, in the classic Albums. What a pleasure to see them
used so successfully in Shirley's original design. With corner
squares commensurately scaled to the rectangular blocks,
these combined elements ring the more substantial central
four blocks in a border-like fashion. The large formal border
beyond them does, indeed, complete this image of grandeur.
(Photo courtesy of Jonathan Chester, Extreme Images)

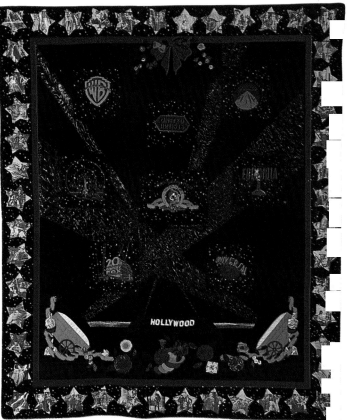

QUILT #40 *(Above, and Detail, above right)*
Katherine L. McKearn. "Allegheny Avenue Album." 1992.
90" x 91". With an artist's confidence, Katherine reincarnates the rather formal antiquarian Baltimore themes with a humorous warmth. Summing up the quilt's persona, she writes, "This is life at our house: nothing fits neatly into its perfect little square!" In a lively and easily understood jargon, this Album eloquently "tells it like it is." The traditional "lightning streak" rhythm is plunked out, electrifying the sashing strips in jagged lines of mother-of-pearl buttons. "These were sewn on in fat times and thin," the varying width of the cloth strips seems to note. The richness of the imagery evokes joy and poignancy in the observer, sure marks of a masterful quilt.

One can imagine the good ladies of bygone Baltimore smiling on this one, thinking they can see a bit into a twentieth-century quiltmaker's soul, as we have seen a bit into theirs. This Album brings a smile to my own thoughts, as well. It is the same contented feeling as comes when I'm in the company of a young family. I remember those days fondly. And I'm happy to be on to tomorrow. The classic Albums have that effect on me, too. I love being in the vicinity of their piety. But I appreciate living freer, living now.

DETAIL: Basket block. A symbol is a visible sign of invisible things. One senses in the classic Baltimore Albums that in general, "baskets hold blessings": fruits, flowers, nuts, birds, books, and butterflies. One could spell further meanings out for each of those symbolic objects, too. But symbols speak directly to the heart, in part because they speak without words. In silence, then, let us savor the symbolic contents of this Allegheny Avenue basket!
(Photos courtesy of James Kharmrodt Lightner)

NOTES ON THE ONE-BLOCK QUILTS (#26-#35)
SHOWN IN THE COLOR SECTION

QUILT #26
Ellen Peters. "Grapevine Lyre." 1990. 20½" x 20½". This is
the first in a series, shown here, in which Ellen has designed
single blocks from *Baltimore Beauties* into decorative wall
quilts. (*Photo courtesy of Ellen Peters*)

QUILT #27
Marlene Peterman. "Appliqué an Heirloom." 1992. 60" x 60".
In a lovely style very much her own, Marlene sets four Album
blocks, centered on a gentle dove and bordered with an
energetic ribbon-threaded rose vine. (*Photo courtesy of Jack
Mathieson*)

QUILT #41 (*Left, previous page*)
Marilyn Norris Hamaker. "Baltimore Goes Hollywood."
1991. 50" x 70". Subtitled, "Crazy About the Movies."
Titularly tied to Baltimore, this elaborately hand appliquéd
quilt is, like its ancestors, an Album of symbols as well as of
appliqués. Its secular symbols evoke the Golden Age of
Hollywood. They are the logos of the major studios that
loomed larger than life on the screens of our childhood. The
border is studded with xerographed stars, echoing and reaf-
firming that favorite symbol since time immemorial. Other
antiquarian motifs, reflected in Baltimore, shine again here:
the bow-tied festoon, the stylized flowers, the cornucopia.
That horn of plenty's symbolism is easily read by all of us who
lived through and loved the movies' greatest era.

   The quilt's set is dramatically innovative. It captures the
studio symbols in dust-sparkled stage lights, perfectly express-
ing these miracles wrought for us, mid-twentieth century. For
our children, these Hollywood symbols may become "just
beyond memory," as so many symbols in the classic Albums
are for us. Then, too, these cinema symbols bespeak the pho-
tographic age just begun, coincident with the Albums, mid-
nineteenth century. Again, what would our needlesisters
think, were they able to see how diversely our admiration for
their quilts has led? In its cultural and technological specificity,
this quilt would be less understandable to antebellum Album
makers than the very human themes, many timeless, of the
Allegheny Avenue Album. But what if the connection were
made, "Remember the daguerreotypes? Remember the big
step when the cameras moved outside to picture buildings and
full outdoor scenes?" Then we would have common ground.
We could explain how our quilts, like theirs, express excitement, wonder, at how light has "become its own historian" in
ever expanding roles. "Then came moving pictures, sound,
color, television, satellite photography, and on and on with no
end in sight. But the 'movies' were best when we were young.
Marilyn is remembering that for us all, in her late twentieth-
century Album Quilt." (*Photo courtesy of Rob Goebel*)

QUILT #28
Donna Bailey. "Sky Flowers." 1990. 26" x 26". Worked on a
"sky-dyed" ground, Donna's Album block has become a beautiful small quilt, its border echoing other Album themes. The use
of specialty fabrics with increasing saturations of color is as old
as antebellum Baltimore, and the effect it creates (of depth in a
quilt) as timeless. It is one of the many echoes of antiquity that
has found such favor in modernist as well as traditionalist contemporary quilts. (*Photo courtesy of Donna Bailey*)

QUILT #29
Ellen Peters. "Fleur-de-Lis." 1990. 15¼" x 15¼". Echoing the
sculptural outline of the Album block, Ellen's cutaway appliqué
border completes this small quilt well. (*Photo courtesy of Ellen
Peters*)

QUILT #30
Claire Jarratt. "Friendship." 1990. 36" x 36". This Album
block (in unusually "old looking" colors) is framed by four
borders that meld patchwork, appliqué, and solid strips of border. Made as an "exchange" Christmas gift for Rosalee Sanders,
the resulting quilt has a highly individual look. (*Photo courtesy
of Sharon Risedorph*)

QUILT #31
Marlene Peterman. "Spring Basket." 1992. 30" x 30".
Marlene's original design focuses here on the basket theme.
Rich color and dimensional flowers bespeak the evolution of
Marlene's style. (*Photo courtesy of Jack Mathieson*)

QUILT #32
Ellen Peters. "Sweetheart Rose Lyre." 1990. 20" x 21".
A white border embellished with quilting and a dark heavy
binding provide a dressy looking finish to this petite, rather
formal wall quilt. (*Photo courtesy of Ellen Peters*)

QUILT #33
Niki Baker. "Baltimore Bouquet." 1990-1991. 31" x 31".
Inspired by pictures of old quilts, Niki designed this richly
colored floral bouquet and bordered it rhythmically with
scalloping swags. (*Photo courtesy of Niki Baker*)

QUILT #34
Ellen Peters. "Crown of Laurel." 1990. 23½" x 23½".
A strong pieced border completes the beloved stylization of the
laurel crown into a one-block quilt. (*Photo courtesy of Ellen
Peters*)

QUILT #35
Ellen Peters. "Feather-Wreathed Heart." 1990. 23½" x 24".
Ellen's original adaptation of the author's *Volume I* pattern,
"Feather-Wreathed Heart with Doves," adds to our heritage of
"feathered" quilt designs. (*Photo courtesy of Ellen Peters*)

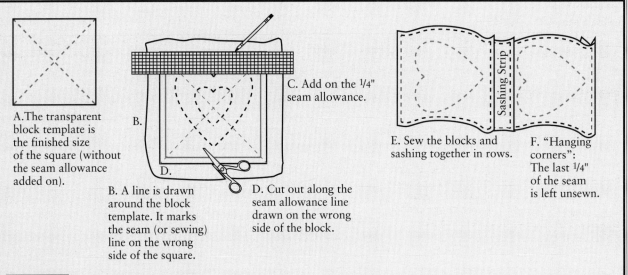

A. The transparent block template is the finished size of the square (without the seam allowance added on).

B. A line is drawn around the block template. It marks the seam (or sewing) line on the wrong side of the square.

C. Add on the ¼" seam allowance.

D. Cut out along the seam allowance line drawn on the wrong side of the block.

E. Sew the blocks and sashing together in rows.

F. "Hanging corners": The last ¼" of the seam is left unsewn.

Picture this:

Cutting the Blocks to Size and Assembling the Block-body Unit

When you've decided the order in which you'll present your blocks, you'll need to trim them all to the same size. All the block patterns in the *Baltimore Beauties* series (and in *Spoken Without a Word*) have a design image for a 12½" block. But often we choose to leave more white space (by using a 14" block, for example) or use patterns from different sources. Before you start, iron the block (face down on a towel). Here's how to assemble the body of blocks:

A. Make a seam-marking template the exact size of the finished square. A transparent plastic square is ideal. Draw diagonal lines on it from corner to corner. When you place this block template on the wrong side of the block you'll be able to see the stitching pattern through it. Carefully center the appliqué design. Use a bit of masking tape to hold the template in place while you draw.

B. Draw around the square. The drawn line is your seam line.

C. Add the ¼" seam allowance beyond it .

D. Cut out the block along this seam allowance line.

E. Assemble the blocks (and sashings if applicable) from top to bottom, in a row.

F. Leave the seams with "hanging corners." Such seams are stitched up to, but not through, the quarter-inch of seam

allowance. This allows the seams to be pressed together in consistent directions after sewing and facilitates setting the block-body unit into a pre-assembled (doughnut-like) border. We'll consider in a moment when preassembling the border makes sense and when it doesn't. (See Figure 14.)

Ponder this:

When all the block-sashing rows are assembled in strips the length of the quilt, you'll then sew these strips to each other, from left to right.

In the antebellum Albums, when no corner blocks are used, there is a recurring pattern that puzzles me. Theoretically, either the horizontal or the vertical sashing could be the sashing all in one piece. But time and again, it is the vertical sashing that runs the length of the quilt, while the horizontal ones are the short pieces, one block long. Study the assembly pattern followed in the quilts pictured in *Volume II's* Quilt Gallery. Do the photos bear out our theory? Why do you suppose such a consistent approach was taken? Was it tradition, practicality, or some other factor? (Just to keep us humble, our front cover quilt marches to a different drummer!)

Making a Master Border Strip Pattern and a Master Border Corner Pattern

A Master Border Pattern enables you to tailor any border to fit your block layout perfectly. Include the finished block size and the width of the finished sashing (if applicable) when you calculate the length of your block-body unit for your Master Border Pattern. The block-body unit is the sewn-together blocks. If sashing is used, that is also part of the block-body unit. (Think the number of sash-ings through carefully: will your sashing frame the out-side row of quilt blocks, or not?) Like all patchwork pat-terns, your Master Border Pattern will be the finished size of the border. The ¼" seams will be added beyond the drawn outline of the pattern when you cut it from back-ground cloth.

If, like me, you are a more visual quiltmaker (as opposed to having sharp math skills), assemble your block-body unit before you make the Master Border

Figure 10A-F.
Making a Master Border Pattern.

A.   The block-body unit is the blocks (and sashings if applicable) sewn together without the border.

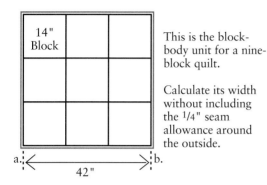

This is the block-body unit for a nine-block quilt.

Calculate its width without including the 1/4" seam allowance around the outside.

B.   The Master Border Strip Pattern (12" x 42") is cut out of freezer paper. It is the width of the border and the finished length of the block-body unit.

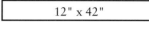

The Master Border Strip Pattern is cut out of freezer paper.

C.   The Master Border Corner Pattern (12" x 12") is cut out of freezer paper. It has been folded in half to mark the diagonal center axis. Make two of these. Leave one whole for a separate-corner block pattern. Cut the second one in half along the diagonal. (The two triangular halves will be used to make a mitered border pattern.)

Making a Master Pattern for a
Square Border Corner
This square plus the Border Strip makes one Master Border Pattern.

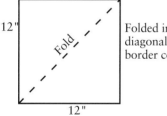

Folded in half to mark the diagonal center axis of the border corner.

D.   **Making a Master Pattern for a Border with Mitered Corners**
Tape the border strip and two half-corner square triangles together to form a pattern for a mitered border.

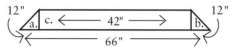

E.   The border corner square pattern is useful in designing a border's appliqués as well. You could also use the diagonal fold in the square Master Corner Border Pattern to help you design a nice bisymmetrical vine-turning border corner, like that on the back cover quilt.

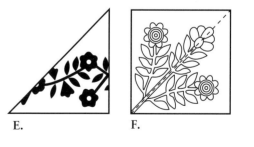

E.   F.

F.   Or you could use the diagonal to help place paper cut-outs of leaves and flowers to replicate the corner bouquets of the front cover quilt.

Pattern (Figure 10). Then you have fewer abstract concepts to deal with on paper or in your head. Moreover, you'll have committed yourself to a final set for the body of the quilt and you'll tailor the color and design of the border, as well as its fit, to the real quilt. Either way, follow the steps illustrated in Figure 10 for making your customized Master Border Pattern.

Fine-tuning Borders
Because *Baltimore Beauties* encourages you to design your own quilt (size, sashing, set, borders), no printed border can be guaranteed to fit. You'll need to test any border pattern for exact fit. To do this, first make your Master Border Pattern as above. This is a pattern custom-tailored to your block-body unit. Write on it what the depth of the border is and what the length of the border strip is. Always make a separate border corner pattern

Figure 11A-J. A Handful of Border Design Motifs.
Border design patterns for three quilts are provided here for you to tailor to your Master Border Strip Pattern and Master Border Corner Pattern.

1. Design elements for the front cover's Sarah Schaefer quilt border (12" deep with one 14" Swag and Blossom repeat per block. The border has a separate flower spray corner block, 12" square.) Their templates here are: D, the large blossom that connects the scalloped swags; H, the scalloped swag (this, combined with a blossom makes a 14" long repeat); A, B, C, and E are the leaf and blossoms that with stem I make the border sprigs. These same four design elements combine to make the border corner block. Use a Dogtooth Triangle edging border from *Volume II* (Pattern #29 or 30). Imagine how showy this deep swag would be cut from a rich large red print.

A.

B.

C.

D.

H.
14" Swag and Blossom Border Repeat

I.

F.

E.

G.
F and G make a 14" Laurel and Swag. Repeat for an 8½" deep border.

Place stem and swags on fold (cut double)

J.

2. Laurel and Swag Border (8" border with a 14" motif repeat). Two design motifs (F and G) make up this border pattern.

3. Reverse Feather Plume Border (9" border with 7" plume repeat). See this in the Border Gallery. This border seems without rival in its lacey opulence. In the antique original (Photo 4-14 in *Volume II*), these plumes are reverse appliquéd from white to red, the only actual appliqué being along the outside curves of the feathers. The quill center of the plume is a fine white soutache braid; the segments of the petal shapes are finely embroidered in white. This sounds like sacrilege, but I wonder if some machine dynamo couldn't do this border pattern with breathtaking elegance, using fine wool machine embroidery thread?

Figure 12A-E. Custom Tailoring a Master Border Pattern.
You can tailor any printed border pattern to fit your own border. Moreover, by the same steps, you can take elements from any block pattern or quilt picture and make them into your own original border pattern.

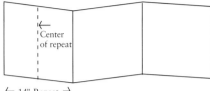

A. Here the Master Border Pattern has been accordion-folded into the desired number (three) of repeats.

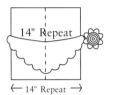 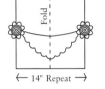

B. When tried on for size, the swag and blossom motif (cut out of single-fold paper) is too big for this repeat. It will have to be reduced.

C. In this case, the adjustment was made by redrawing the design on folded paper and cutting it out. (You can also photo-reduce the pattern, or draw it smaller.)

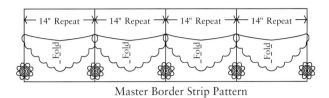

Master Border Strip Pattern

D. This shows a swag motif stack-cut and laid onto the Master Border Strip Pattern to see if it repeats a whole number of times. It does, but it's clearly too big. There's no room between the swags for the blossom part of the motif. On the other hand, it looks promising. The great virtue of paper-cuts is that they can give you other ideas. I can see a charmingly plump "folk art" heart, here, reverse appliquéd out of each swag. A smaller such heart appliquéd on top could link the swags. Or perhaps the swags could be left this close and an elegant knotted tassel could be appliquéd over each juncture.

E. If all you need is a minimal size change, you can simply tailor your original pattern. Adjust the ends of the motif, or cut it in half to adjust the center by (a) taping an extension behind its center or (b) overlapping the two pattern halves to reduce it. You'll need to recut or redraw the top and bottom curves smooth again (c).

and label its depth and width. The issue for running borders (border designs that run contiguously across the quilt) is whether the basic motif unit (one swag and blossom unit, for example) repeats a whole number of times the length of the border strip. The length of one full border motif is called its "repeat." This is often labeled on the pattern. Figure 13 shows how to design a border using the Master Border Pattern.

Using the Master Pattern to Design a Border
With a paper template cut the size of the finished border, a wealth of border designs lies at your fingertips. An easy approach is to fold your Master Pattern into an even number of units and work out a design for one unit, or for two of these units combined (Figure 13A). I like to do this with papercutting. I use white paper (scrap or freezer paper) to cut my first few tries. You could cut separate fruit and leaf motifs, for instance, and arrange them on a twining stem within two of these units. Repeated, these would make a running border.

Try laying the vine stem out initially in heavy white yarn tacked with removable tape. It's a quick way to cap-

ture a style (Figure 13B). When the contiguous papercut design motifs are cut from white paper, this white yarn vine helps you visualize the finished design. If it appeals, trace the rough design right onto the border pattern. This is your "rough draft." You can fine-tune it onto another Master Border Pattern (Figure 13C). The feather plume border on the front cover inspired my "Dancing Grapevine Border" from Quilt #17 in *Volume II.* Both these borders have irregular repeats and had to be designed as full (or at least half) borders. In the case of the grapevine, I laid it out just as described.

There are several classic Album Quilts that use discrete (nontouching) motifs placed in a regular, rhythmic pattern across the border (Figure 13D). These are assorted leaves, a repeated posey, or a fern frond as in Photo 4-22 in *Volume II.* Stack-cut such motifs of paper, first, and lay them out on your Master Border Pattern.

Your *Baltimore Beauties* books are treasuries of design motifs. If you want a formal flower sprig to repeat along the border, or a folk art blossom to unite your swags, just trace those right off one of the patterns. If you want arboreal leaves marching around your border, all tilted into

Figure 13A-D. Design a Border with your Master Border Pattern.

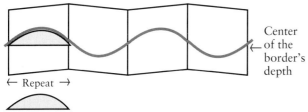

C. Trace as many repeats of the finished design as you need onto your Master Border Pattern. You'll design the corner now, in much the same way. To translate the design to fabric, you'll need the vine shape drawn the length of the border strip, then templates for the leaves, and a freezer-paper strip pattern for the edging borders if they're to be included. If I were to do the rather succulent looking vine (C), I'd cut out the leaves and stem as one freezer paper pattern, iron it onto a strip of green, and do the entire border by cutaway appliqué.

A. Fold your Master Border Pattern into an even number of units. To make a vine, cut a shallow curve template that will fit within one unit. Reverse it in the next unit and so on. Lay a temporary "vine" of string or bulky white yarn to follow the sketchy template line and attach it with removable tape.

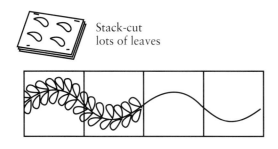

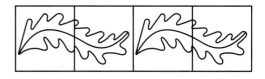

B. Stack-cut leaves from the template and arrange them along two or three repeats. If you like its look, trace this vine/leaf mock-up onto your pattern. Try an edging border if your quilt body can take a widened border.

D. Separate motif borders are fun and so easy! Here's a rendition of an antique one.

the wind at the same angle, go pick them up off your front lawn, or from a place that is meaningful to you. (For me, leaves from Mount Vernon are a pleasant thought!) Enlarge them, reduce them, or repeat one just as you trace it.

Using the Master Pattern to Design a Corner
Corners can be turned by tailoring the design motif to bend around the corner attractively. I have a personal preference for corners whose patterned image dips towards the outside edge of the border, thus opening the quilt up. I designed the border corners of Quilt #6 and #7 in *Volume I* to work this way.

You have three major design approach choices regarding corners:

1. Corners can continue the border design motif.

2. They can do this without a break in a running border, or they can continue the basic design but break at the corners (the Updegraf Feather Border on the cover does the latter).

3. They can be distinct, separate design units like those on the Sarah Shaefer front cover quilt. See also Border I. #3

in the Border Gallery. This uses one element of the border design and changes the rest dramatically. In Border I. #4 in the Border Gallery, the corners act as complete and separate block designs. Again, in Photos 4-13 and 4-22 from *Volume II*, the corners are radically different from the border. Use your separate Master Border Corner Pattern to design a fine corner for your border.

Border Lessons
If you don't have the time to do each exercise, simply researching the references and then visualizing a solution to the design issue posed will teach you a great deal. It will get you thinking creatively about borders.

Figure 14A-D. Allowing for Appliqué Shrinkage.

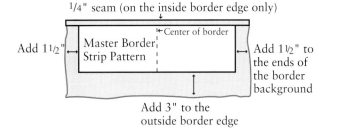

A. You may need to compensate for appliqué shrinkage when you cut the initial border background yardage. Cut the borders larger to begin with, and then tailor them to size for assembly. Add the adjustment allowance noted to every edge except the inside edge of the border. (There, you'll draw the pattern line for the inside border edge and simply add the 1/4" seam beyond it. Also mark the center point of the border top and bottom. These are your fixed points for when you use the Master Border Pattern, once again, to cut the border to size after the appliqué is done.) Add more (3" allowance) to the outside edge of the border strip in case you end up self-binding the quilt.

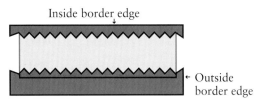

B. Add this adjustment allowance to the outside edging border fabric (if you are using one) as well.

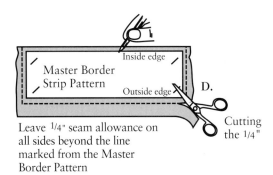

C. After the finished appliqué has been ironed, pin the Master Border Strip on to the wrong side of the border. Draw a pencil line all around this pattern.

D. Trim back to 1/4" seam allowance all around. The exception is the outside border edge if you are going to mock-bind the border. For mock binding, see Figure 17.

Lesson 15: Peas in a Pod

Goal: To choose a repeated block whose motif is echoed in the border.

Exercise. Pick up some element of the repeat center block and use it as a border element, either to make a corner block for the border of your choice, or to incorporate in the length of the border. (See Quilt #7 in *Volume I*.)

Lesson 16: Three's Company

Goal: To see how easy it is to make a custom-designed swag border pattern.

Exercise A. Design just three repeats of your own swag border motif. Design the border pattern by choosing a swag (a one-layer swag or two, or three-layered? A smooth or scallop-edged swag?) and a connector (a bow, a flower, a star, a figure, etc.). Design it in the way that comes most easily to you: by tracing or drawing, or by tracing, drawing, and papercutting.

Exercise B. Design a border corner to go with the swag border motif you've just designed. Design it to attach to that original border design.

Exercise C. Design a detached border corner block. Choose a motif from a traditional border (a flower, a bow, etc.). Use that motif as a design element in making your original corner for that border. Design a block, separate from that border. (An example is the antique quilt on this book's front cover.)

Lesson 17: In the Spotlight

Goal: To experiment with the potential of a Master Border Pattern on a small scale, and to design a frame for a single block to make it into a showy wall quilt.

Exercise A. After you've played with sketching, make a paper Master Pattern to scale for an 18" block. (An 18" block could be a 14"-16" block with an inner frame of sashing around it.) Cut the freezer paper border patterned 18" x 7" (unless you prefer another width). Make a border corner pattern with a 7" square folded on the diagonal. Try a variety of design approaches to see what works for you. Fold the length of the border into an accordion of regular width units.

Exercise B. Design a vine border for this hypothetical one-block wall hanging. Lay a piece of bulky yarn or string out to play with the vine style. Use a flexible ruler (from an art store) to draw the vine for just half the length of the border on a separate piece of white paper. Cut this length of vine out and stick it to your Master Pattern with a repositionable glue-stick. Stack cut leaves (or buds, flowers, fruit) out of white paper and position them on the Master Pattern. The shapes need to please you before you consider color. Separate each issue so that the process does not seem overwhelming. One step at a time.

Exercise C. Experiment with your options: Do you want this vine border to have a center focus? Do you want it to break completely in the center to continue gracefully again on the other side? Do you want different vines on two sides of the quilt? On three sides of the quilt? Do you want inner borders and/or edging borders?

Exercise D. If this vine border has caught your imagination, design a corner for it. Consider echoing the border center vine shape (if it is different) in the border corner shape. If "the vine" has not yet caught your imagination, forget the corner—and the entire vine border for now. Designing vine borders may not be your thing. Or, in that wonderful way that creativity works, inspiration may come later.

Figure 15A-C. Assembling Borders.

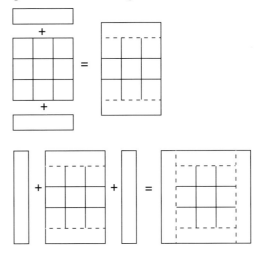

A. The patchwork path of assembling a four-piece border to the block-body of the quilt.

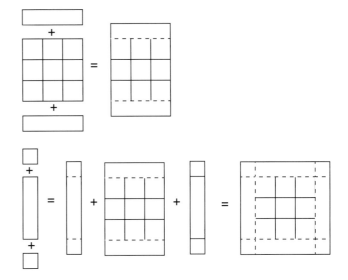

B. The patchwork path of assembling a border (with separate corner blocks) to the block-body unit of the quilt.

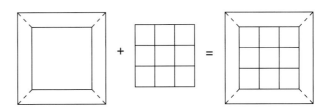

C. The patchwork path of setting a block-body unit into a pre-assembled border frame. The secret is to leave "hanging corners" on the seams—especially where the four corners of the quilt block unit are set into the four corners of the frame unit.

Lesson 18: Gilding the Lily

Goal: To enhance an already appealing quilt set with a border.

Exercise A. Pick your favorite quilt paste-up from previous lessons and make it even prettier with the perfect border.

Exercise B. Make a mock-up that closely resembles the quilt you are working on. Choose and paste on the border that at this point seems best to suit both your personality and the quilt.

Sewing on the Border

When cutting the background fabric for the borders, add 3" total (1½" at each end) to the Master Border Pattern's length and 3" total (along the outside edge) to its width. (See Figure 14A.) This, which we'll call the "adjustment allowance," provides for any shrinkage from the appliqué process itself. Add this adjustment allowance to the raw edge of outside edging border appliqués. (See Figure 14B.) There it can either be trimmed back at the end, or sewn as a "mock binding" that binds the quilt from front to back.

Do the appliqué, putting on edging border designs before center-running ones. Simply baste the edging appliqué that runs into the "adjustment allowance" at either end of the border strip. Some of this will be trimmed off, so don't appliqué the ends down until (when all the other appliqué is complete) you have cut the borders to final size. In some cases you will finish these juncture appliqués after you have joined the border units. This way you can fine tune the connections, during or after the seaming process.

When the appliqué is complete, press the borders face down on a towel. Optional: You may spray starch it from the back. (Test your fabric first.) Stiffening the border makes marking around the large Master Border Pattern a bit easier. Pin the Master Pattern to the back of the border strip. Add ¼" seams around the Master Border Pattern (and border corner if made separately). (See Figure 14C-D.) Cutting the border to final patchwork size after 99% of the appliqué is done compensates for any appliqué shrinkage.

The big question, when the appliqué is all done, is: Do you sew the whole border first like a doughnut, then add the quilt? When sewing borders onto the quilt, it makes much more sense to add the top and bottom borders first; next you would add the longer side borders. (See Figure 15A.) If your border has corner blocks, make one long rectangular unit by attaching the corner squares at either end of the border strips. (See Figure 15B.)

The stumbling block in an appliqué border comes with those running border designs (both edge and/or center running). One has to make the appliqué from one border unit fit like a seamless stocking to the appliqué on the next border unit. The difficulty can be exaccerbated when the appliqué (an edging border, for example) becomes part of the border's seam at a corner. If the appliqué is complex, or if the border corners are mitered, I would pre-assemble the whole border as a big doughnut-like unit. Then I could tailor those meddlesome corner appliqués before the block unit makes it too cumbersome to handle easily. When the border is to your taste, add the quilt to fill in the hole in the center (Figure 15C).

To "set in" a quilt, you need to stop the sewing on your seams ¼" before the raw edge. Some people call this "hanging corners." Setting a square into a border corner is similar to setting in a gusset in dressmaking. What are your other options? Some borders leave a small appliqué unit that is added on top of the border after the corner is seamed. Be careful you don't forget it as we did on one corner in Quilt #8 in *Volume I*! Another possibility is to sew the appliqué down on one unit but leave it unsewn for a few inches on the next border unit. After the two are seamed together, you can appliqué the loose shape to join the other to perfection. In point of fact, there are no rules. Assess your particular border and ask yourself which approach suits your personality. Knowing what the problems might be, is to be well on the way to the solution.

Finishing Touches

Quilting Advice

Volume II explores how the classic Albums were quilted. The papercutting of quilting motifs ties in nicely here for those who might enjoy custom designing their quilting.

Versatile freezer paper can be a boon to the quilting process. Shapes cut out of it can be ironed tightly to the finished quilt top before it is basted out. These shapes are left on and quilted around with no further marking needed. (See Figure 16.) Simply peel off the pattern when finished. (If it resists lifting, rewarm it with an iron to loosen.) This disposable pattern in itself solves the major hurdle of getting rid of all marking lines when the quilting is done.

There are further wonders to designing quilting in freezer paper. You can stack-cut your motifs (staple four layers of freezer paper together) and iron one in every place you will use it. This helps you visualize what the quilting will look like before you're committed to it. You can fine-tune placement and think about what background quilting you will use.

As a general rule, appliquéd Album Quilts are either quilted entirely in "filler patterns" or they have individual quilted motifs (flowers, leaves, feather plumes, sprays) with filler patterns in the space between these motifs and the appliquéd motifs. The filler patterns are repeated patterns made by straight or curved lines in geometric configurations. Additional "white space"

Figure 16A-C. Freezer Paper Quilting Templates.
Did you know you can quilt around an ironed-down freezer paper template?

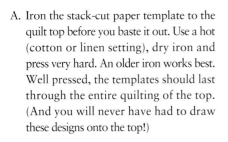

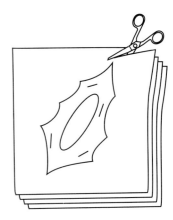

A. Iron the stack-cut paper template to the quilt top before you baste it out. Use a hot (cotton or linen setting), dry iron and press very hard. An older iron works best. Well pressed, the templates should last through the entire quilting of the top. (And you will never have had to draw these designs onto the top!)

B. Use a simple filler pattern behind your representation motifs. Here 1/2"-wide drafting tape was used to mark parallel lines spaced 1/2" apart.

C. If you have really good strong sharp scissors, you can stack-cut your templates and speed up the process. I've cut up to eight layers of freezer paper with a clean sharp design edge. Mark the quilting shape on the top layer. Staple in two or three places within the template design area, and cut. Pre-test your scissors. There's no savings if you try to cut more layers than they can handle.

solutions are simply echoing the appliqués in close rows of quilting, or stippling (a tight, closely filled-in quilting whose pattern may become almost random).

To me, the most exciting aspect of using freezer paper for quilting motifs is the design freedom it gives you in the motifs themselves. There are all the possibilities of folded papercut designs, folk motifs, and traditional quilting designs. Additionally, because designs can be traced and cut, the whole world of possible quilt designs widens. In the quilt "Classic Revival Album," in *Volume III*, I made an acorn and oak leaf pattern, using leaves from our Hamilton family's ancestral farm in West Virginia. In actual fact, I designed a limited number of graceful oak sprays from the leaves, then stack-cut them out of freezer paper. After placing them carefully and ironing them down, I sent the "marked" top with a filler pattern diagram (and 1/4" and 1/2" drafting tape to mark the straight quilting lines) off to West Virginia, where a long-time family friend, Mona Cumberledge and her daughter, Joyce Hill, quilted it.

Three Antebellum Bindings
The binding is the last step in making a quilt. It follows the quilting process, anchors the three layers of a quilt (the top, the batting, the backing) together, and binds them securely. Binding can also be an important player in the color design of a quilt. And where it has been done with style, it is the kind of exquisite detail that raises a beautiful quilt right up to masterpiece level.

Let's look at Mock Binding (self-binding), the Upedgraf Binding (a piped and scalloped edge), and the Beehive Binding (piped and tucked fabric bound flat toward the interior of the quilt).

A. Mock Binding: Quilts can be bound using the top fabric, seaming it, and pulling it to the back. Or the same approach can be reversed: the backing fabric is pulled to the front. The mock binding is a seamed binding and gives a very fine tight edge to the quilt. The binding itself is double-layered and so very durable. The following are measurements to use with one of the lower loft polyester batts, or with a thin cotton batt.

To mock bind with the top fabric, leave an additional 1 1/2" of fabric beyond where the border would ordinarily end. (In Figure 17A, it is the edging appliqué fabric that provides the extra 1 1/2" needed for the binding. The outer edge of the white border fabric would have been trimmed back to the outside edge of the quilt.)

1. Fold this 1 1/2" back in half lengthwise and press it back against the border. Line the raw edge up with the first fold to make the "binding" (Figure 17A).

2. Pin this binding and the three layers of the quilt together. Place the pins perpendicular to the raw edge so that you can pass over them when you machine stitch (Figure 17B).

3. Stitch the binding and the three layers of the quilt together, making a fine 1/4" seam. Leave the last 1/2" of the seam unstitched at the corner, "hanging" (Figure 17C).

Figure 17A-E. Mock Binding.

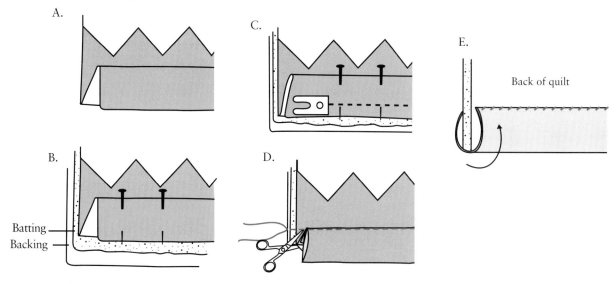

4. Carefully trim the excess batting and backing off to the edge of the top (the raw edge of the seam). Next pull the binding forward against the machined seam and around to the back of the quilt (Figure 17D). The look you're after is a tiny binding on the front. If there's any leeway, make it a smidgin wider on the back.

5. Hand appliqué the binding to the back of the quilt, using the tack stitch (Figure 17E). Hand finish the corners.

B. The Updegraf Binding: To make a sample scalloped edging, use the scallop template. Stack-cut the template shape out of a 15" accordion-folded strip of freezer paper. Next iron it onto the wrong side of a 2" x 15" rectangle of red cotton. This paper marks your sewing line on the scalloped side and the place to add your 1/4" seam on the straight side.

1. Pin the paper-marked red fabric (right sides together) with a second same-sized red rectangle (Figure 18B).

2. Machine stitch the scallops. Sew right next to, but not through, the paper. Note that there is a short 1/3" reverse curve at the bottom of each scallop. Back-stitch this once before proceeding forward. Trim off the seam to 3/16"; clip to, but not into, the back-stitching. Turn the first few scallops right side out. If the seam seems bulky, go back and cut one of the seams back to 1/8" to grade the seams. Make evenly spaced clips, two-thirds

of the way through the 3/16" seam (Figure 18C).

3. Turn the scalloped edging right side out and press from the back.

4. Prepare the tiny yellow piping, using a scant 1/8" diameter cord, nestled in the long fold of a 3/4" strip of yellow (Figure 18D).

5. Pin this piping strip, raw edges together, to the length of the 15" strip of border, front side up (Figure 18E). Seam the piping to the border with a 3/16" seam.

6. Lay the scallop strip on the table. Turn the border with piping strip over on top of it, so that you're looking at the wrong side of the border and can see the stitches where you sewed on the piping. Line all the raw edges up together and pin. Next sew border, piping, and scallop together using a 1/4" seam. This means your stitches will go just to the interior side of the previous stitches. Keep very close to the previous stitches so you don't catch the piping (Figure 18F).

7. Now assemble the block-body and the border. Baste out the quilt. Quilt it. When that is done, hand-press the scallop and piping away from the quilt, as in Figure 18A (front view). To finish, trim the batt back to the edge of the scalloped edging's raw edge. Trim the backing back 1/2" beyond that and hem it to the seam-line along the scallops as in the back view of Figure 18A.

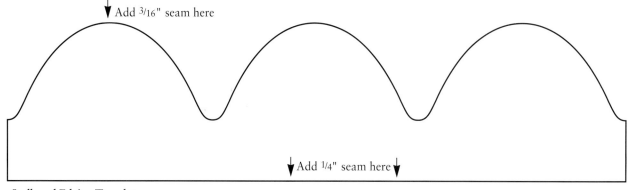

Scalloped Edging Template

Figure 18A-F. Updegraf Binding.

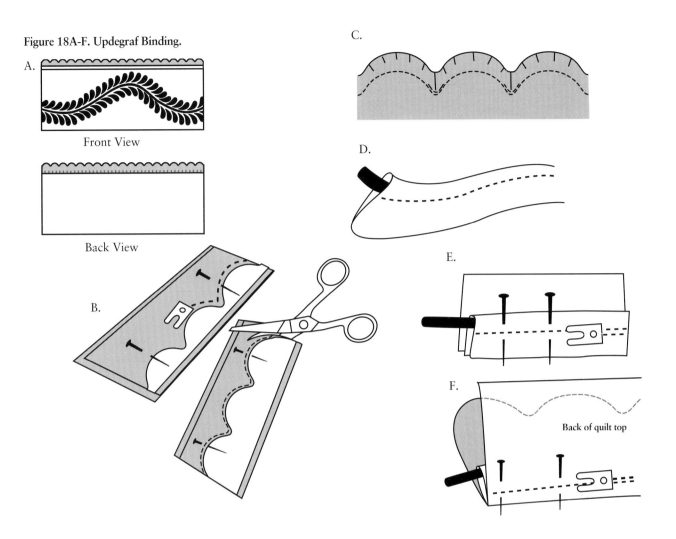

Front View

Back View

C. The Beehive Binding: Here a tiny fold of red lies between the green piping and the border proper. Both are pressed toward the body of the quilt and bound in red. So that you can follow these directions more easily, parts of this three-piece edging are labeled by color as well as name and measurements. It would probably be a good idea to baste the red "tuck" and the green piping to the border first, before pinning on the binding and machine sewing the 1/4" seam. Do all this before the quilt is basted out. The beauty of this edge would be lost if it were all wavy and uneven.

After the quilting is finished, sew through the binding seam a second time, this time joining all the layers of the "quilt sandwich" together. Trim the batting and backing. Pull the binding from front to back and hand-hem to the back. The front should be a masterpiece of elegant proportion, as illustrated (Figure 19B).

Figure 19A-B. Beehive Binding.

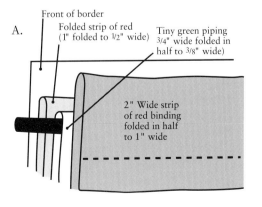

A.

Front of border

Folded strip of red (1" folded to 1/2" wide)

Tiny green piping 3/4" wide folded in half to 3/8" wide)

2" Wide strip of red binding folded in half to 1" wide

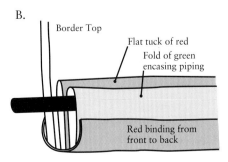

B.

Border Top

Flat tuck of red

Fold of green encasing piping

Red binding from front to back

PHOTO 4. MEDALLION-CENTERED ALBUM QUILT.

Full bed-sized summer spread in Turkey red, Victoria green, and acrimony orange. Mid- to late-nineteenth century. Provenance unknown. Bought by the author at Quilt America! in Indianapolis.

Defined as collections on a theme, Album Quilts do not follow a rigid presentation format. While the Album Quilts of mid-nineteenth-century Maryland were most frequently made of same-sized squares, set square, numerous variations abound. One such is the medallion-centered Album. Here the center block, a delightfully simple stylized basket of flowers, focuses a collection dominated by "yo-yo" posies that clearly enchanted the maker. The edging borders (triangles, diamonds, squares, scallops) echo design elements in the Baltimores, as does the wool embroidery and the innovative dimensionality of so many of the flowers.

No origin or background information has been conveyed with this quilt. While unfortunate, this encourages the imagination. I picture this as a "country Album" as opposed to the urbane classic Baltimore Albums, offspring of a sophisticated and prosperous mercantile city. There is no elegant imported chintz or rainbow fabric in this quilt. Nor is there any pretension. It simply seems the charming artwork of a creative free spirit. The borders of stark leaves, emerging buds, and full-bloomed sprigs (each in intentional congregations) can be seen on more sophisticated Albums tied more closely to Baltimore. These borders always puzzle me, seeming somewhat "unfinished." Yet they occur repeatedly so that they seem intended to convey some significance lost to the modern viewer. Above all, this particular Album seems a joyful quilt. A somewhat more elegant quilt follows in the Pattern Section. That one, whose full pattern is given, seems carefully pre-planned, equally as full of spirit as the one pictured here, but much more formally presented. (*Photo courtesy of Sharon Risedorph*)

Part Three: The Patterns

The "Heart-Garlanded Album" is most romantic, but it may also be the most approachable of the classic Baltimore-style Albums. Make it yours. Consider forming a study group or sewing circle for this. Perhaps it will help to plan its completion in anticipation of an important celebration. Or make it to remember or to honor someone. (In fact, its symbolism can equally be interpreted with those connotations.) By hand, the top might take an efficient year, working on it most weekday evenings. To have faithfully reproduced this classic quilt will be the experience of a lifetime.

The pattern is taken from a mid-nineteenth-century Baltimore-style Album. A photo of that love-worn original is on page 8 in *Volume II*. The entire pattern for the whole quilt is right here. You are given two complete sets of patterns. One is for a full-sized quilt (a 12½" block image to be sewn onto a block that finishes 13½" square). The second pattern set is for a miniature (a 6¼"

appliqué image to be sewn—or fused—on your block).

If you need detailed help with the pattern transfer or the appliqué, *Volume I* will give you all you need to know. Use the drawing of the quilt to see how many of each block to make and how to place each one. You could do this quilt in just one green, one red, and one blue. Or you can vary your prints and shades within appealing boundaries. I picked a handful of greens and reds, roses, and blues to mix together for our back cover quilt, which was set and machine quilted by Rhondi Hindman.

If you'd like to enrich your own version of this quilt with the kind of ornate inked banderoles and inscriptions seen in *Volume I, Pattern Companion*, see *Volume II* for both those designs and how to do that inkwork. For added elegance, consider cutting quilting motifs from freezer paper, and edging your heirloom quilt with the museum-quality layered red and green Beehive Binding.

The Heart-Garlanded Album (left). (Set *your* quilt any way your heart desires.)

Pattern #1. Border from the Heart-Garlanded Album. Pattern for 10" wide border.

Flop and repeat →

← This line connects corner to border repeat

Delete when flipped to match other side of corner block

↓ Cut and separate to extend to 10" ↓

↑ This line
connects corner
to border repeat

This line marks the diagonal center of the border's corner

Pattern #1. Border from the Heart-Garlanded Album.
Pattern for miniature.

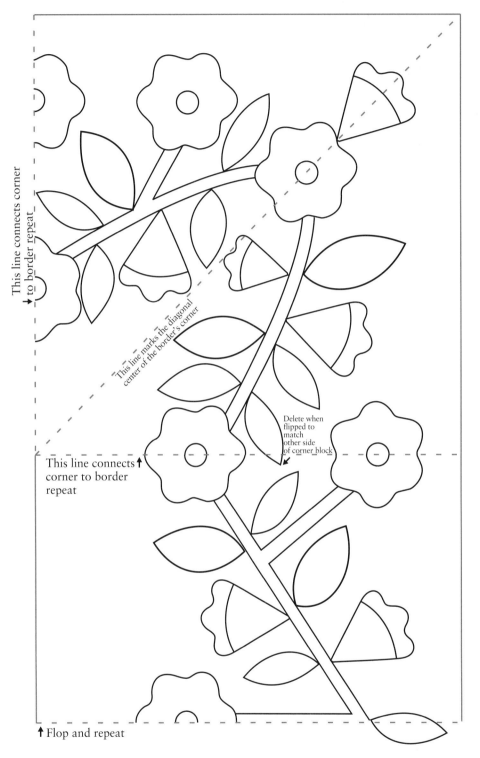

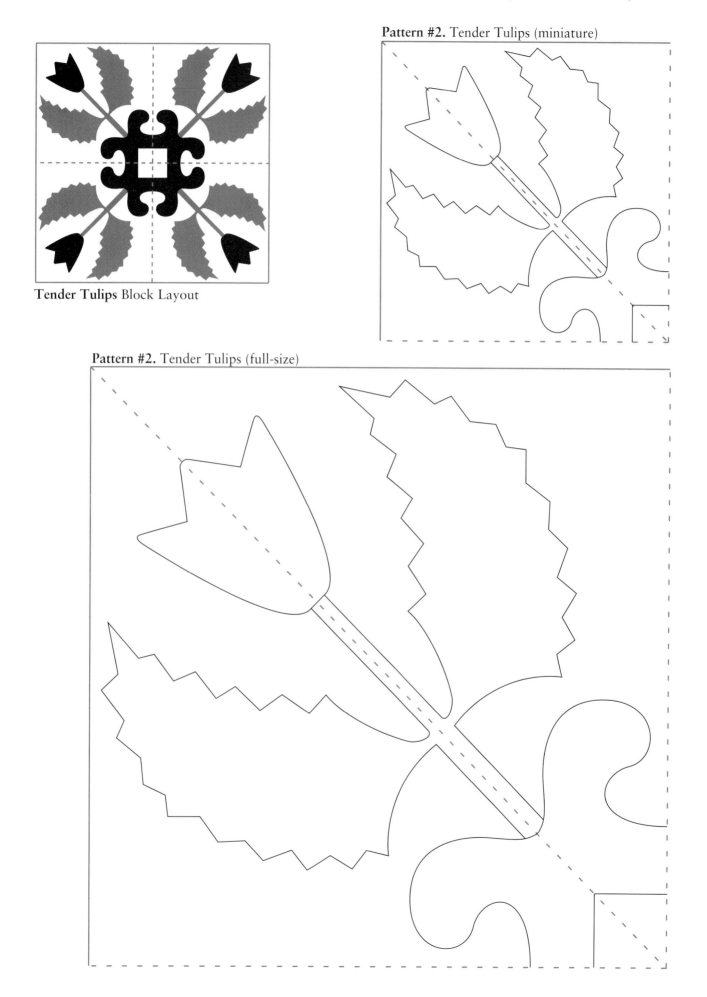

Tender Tulips Block Layout

Pattern #2. Tender Tulips (miniature)

Pattern #2. Tender Tulips (full-size)

Pattern #3. Fleur-de-Lis with Maple Leaves
(miniature)

Fleur-de-Lis with Maple Leaves
Block Layout

Pattern #3. Fleur-de-Lis with Maple Leaves (full-size)

Cactus Flower Block Layout

Pattern #4. Cactus Flower (miniature)

Pattern #4. Cactus Flower (full-size)

Pattern #5. Linked Poseys (miniature)

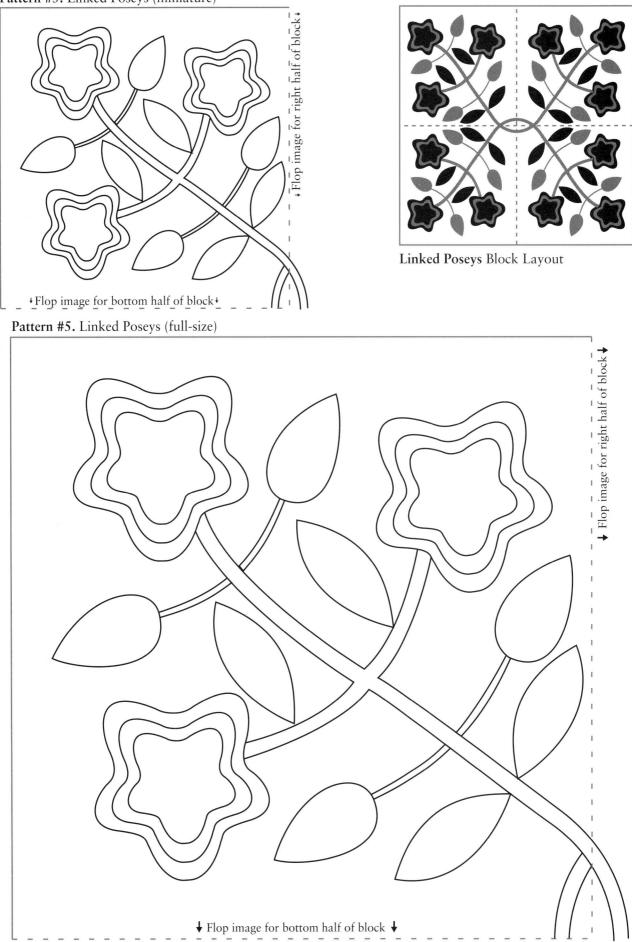

↓Flop image for right half of block↓

↓Flop image for bottom half of block↓

Linked Poseys Block Layout

Pattern #5. Linked Poseys (full-size)

→ Flop image for right half of block →

↓ Flop image for bottom half of block ↓

Pattern #6. Heart Wreath with Buds (miniature)

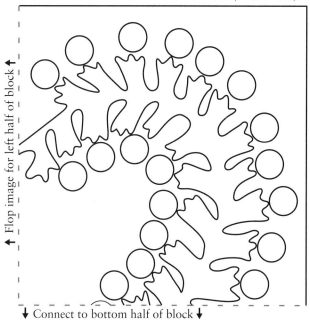

↑ Flop image for left half of block ↑

↓ Connect to bottom half of block ↓

Pattern #6. Heart Wreath with Buds (full-size)

↑ Flop image for left half of block ↑

↓ Connect to bottom half of block ↓

Pattern #6. Heart Wreath with Buds (miniature)
↑ Connect to top half of block ↑

↑ Flop image for left half of block ↑

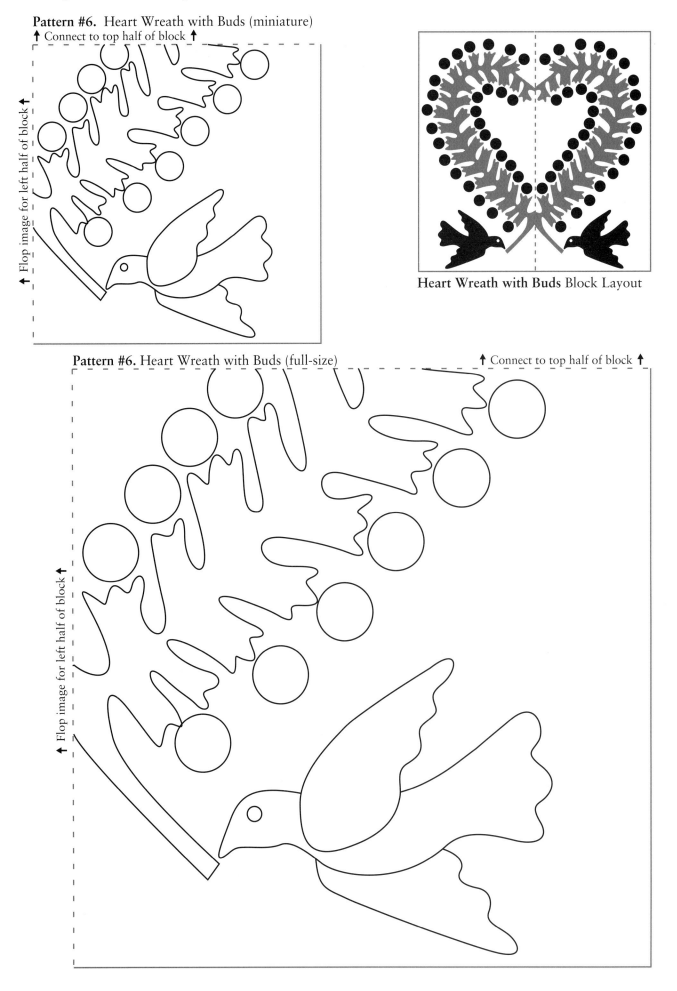

Heart Wreath with Buds Block Layout

Pattern #6. Heart Wreath with Buds (full-size)   ↑ Connect to top half of block ↑

↑ Flop image for left half of block ↑

Part Four: The Needleartists

About the Needleartists whose work appears in *Design a Baltimore Album Quilt! A Design Companion to Baltimore Beauties and Beyond, Volume II.*

When a quiltmaker has offered to contribute stitchery time, talent, or a photo of her piece to the *Baltimore Beauties* series, she fills out a short questionnaire for the series' archival notebooks. The following short biographies are taken from material thus provided. Note: Biographical notes on needleartists generally appear only once in the series even though their work may appear in several volumes.

DONNA BAILEY, Glastonbury, Connecticut. Sky Flowers.

A quilting teacher and lover of appliqué for many years, Donna's original work has won her many ribbons. Taught hand-sewing by her grandmother, Donna particularly enjoys appliqué, writing, "Fabric on fabric, color on color, it's an artform to be shared."

NIKI BAKER, St. Leonard, Maryland. Baltimore Bouquet.

Born and raised in Washington, D.C., and currently living on the family horse farm in southern Maryland, Niki trained as an artist and interior designer. She began quiltmaking in 1975 and began teaching it in 1981. The Baltimore style appeals to her because of its sophisticated fabric use, and the freedom and creativity encouraged by the designs.

KAREN BROWN BLUDORN, Erlanger, Kentucky. Dances with Flowers.

"I love roses, and other flowers, and have grown them for as long as I can remember." Karen notes that in appliqué, her love of flowers melds with a love for fabric. She credits her small quilting circle (with whom she stitches regularly) with inspiring her appliqué quilts. "These friends challenged and encouraged me to produce quilts and to teach appliqué." Karen's seven young children (ages 4 to 15) joke that quilting is her "eighth baby."

DOLORES SMITH BROCK, Yuma, Arizona. Baltimore Album–Yuma Style.

"I was taught to sew by my mother when I was very young. I started quilting ten years ago and find it very relaxing. This quilt won Viewers' Choice at the 1992 Desert Lily Quilt Show. I belong to the Desert Lily Quilters and the Arizona Quilters Guild."

MARIAN K. BROCKSCHMIDT, Springfield, Illinois. Martha's Baltimore and Beyond. Kevin and Jami's Wedding Baltimore and Beyond.

"Winner of the Best of Show in the Mountain Mist 1985 contest, I have become addicted to making Baltimore Beauties and Beyond. I am now on my fourth Album quilt. The freezer paper on-the-top method is my favorite way to appliqué."

LISA BYERS, Water Mill, New York. Design and production coordinator for the Ladies Auxiliary of Water Mill, New York's group quilt, Discovery Quilt.

The Ladies Auxiliary of Water Mill has created a raffle quilt to support the Water Mill Museum for many years. When the Museum wanted to create a special piece in honor of the anniversary of Columbus's voyage, Lisa, having just returned from Elly's Album Quilt workshop on Long Island, became the enthusiastic director of this one-year-long project. Lisa worked for some time as a registered nurse and a Lamaze-trained childbirth educator. With three children (ages 15, 11, and 6) she designs, teaches at the local quilt shop, and is "extremely thankful for my wonderful husband, who allows me the freedom to pursue my quilting dreams!"

MAUREEN CARLSON, Moline, Illinois. Design and production coordinator for the Mississippi Valley Quilters Guild group quilt, Wreaths, Roses, and Ribbons.

The Mississippi Valley Quilters Guild is a bi-state group of over 400 members. This is a raffle quilt for the 1993 National Quilting Association show which they will host in Davenport, Iowa. All fabric used in this project is 100% cotton and was hand dyed by guild members. The block flowers were adapted to represent Iowa and Illinois state flowers: Iowa's Wild Rose and Illinois's Meadow Violet.

KIM CHURBUCK, Country House Cottons, Fayette, Iowa. Album Quilt Label for Wreaths, Roses, and Ribbons.

Kim's love for Victorian detail and handwork are apparent in her exquisite hand-drawn quilt labels. She and Milly Churbuck operate a small hand-dyes and hand-drawn quilt label business (see Appendix II). They are the kind of creative, energetic entrepreneurs whom social history must surely recognize as having nourished the late twentieth century's quilt revival.

MIMI DIETRICH, Catonsville, Maryland. Coordinator for the Baltimore Heritage Quilt Guild's raffle quilt, 1990 Baltimore Album Quilt.

"The quilt was made as a raffle quilt to earn money for our guild, but many of us took part in the project because of the historical significance—just wanting to make stitches on a genuine Baltimore Album quilt!" Mimi herself has had an astonishing influence in the greater Baltimore area, teaching hundreds of students quiltmaking in the Baltimore style. Several "generations" now of Album classes have followed her from Lesson One in *Baltimore Beauties, Volume I,* on through to a myriad of quite wonderful finished quilts. Mimi's students carry her opening day gift to them: a canvas totebag labeled "I'm making my Baltimore Album at the Seminole Sampler Quilt Shop."

JUNE DIXON, Arthur, Illinois. 745th Tank Battalion Album Quilt.

"This quilt was made for my husband Robert Dixon who was a member of the 745th Tank Batallion which was attached to the First Division (The Big Red One) in England before crossing the English Channel on D-Day in World War II and then fighting their way across Europe until the end of the war. Much research on the 745th Tank Batallion was used and symbolism appropriate to their courage and accomplishments was included in the blocks. There are many Army division insignia, also that of the Veterans of Foreign Wars. The star in the border was on all mechanized equipment for identification."

LINDA HALPIN, Horseheads, New York. Appliqué a la Mode.

Linda has been generous in sharing her considerable quiltmaking and design talents as a teacher and writer (once Editor of *Traditional Quiltmaking,* she recently authored her first book, *Patches of Time*). "I began making doll clothes when I was six years old, and haven't stopped sewing since. What began as teaching quiltmaking in my home seventeen years ago has grown into travelling throughout the U.S. and Canada with my classes."

MARILYN NORRIS HAMAKER, Indianapolis, Indiana. Baltimore Sampler. Baltimore Goes Hollywood!

A longtime artist and needleworker, Marilyn has been designing and making quilts since 1981 and considers fabric her favorite "medium." She also enjoys counted thread work and miniature making.

ANITA HARDWICK, Crawfordsville, Indiana. My Country Garden.

Anita's love for textiles began with their use at a very young age. Her first appliqué, a bed covering for her doll, was done at age seven. With so many in the current quilt revival, she became a serious quiltmaker and quilt teacher in 1978.

BETSY HARRIS, Ronsville, Indiana. Delusions of Baltimore.

Betsy is a full-time feature writer at the *Indianapolis Star* and a contributing editor of *Quilter's Newsletter Magazine.* Quiltmaking and quilt-related activities fill her leisure hours.

RHONDI HINDMAN, Walnut Creek, California. Stitching of the Heart-Garlanded Reproduction Baltimore Album Quilt on the back cover.

Rhondi's professional life is replete with quiltmaking, which fills much of her leisure hours as well. She co-manages the mail-order department at the Cotton Patch, teaches a variety of quilt classes there, and is a featured model maker for C & T Publishing's burgeoning trunk shows, project exhibits for their books.

EVELINE (EVE) HOWES, Charlotte, North Carolina. Johannesburg and Beyond.

"I have sewn since childhood and took my first quilting class in 1979 in South Africa, but my work as a pharmacist did not allow much time to pursue this new interest. In 1985 our family moved to the U.S. and with that came the opportunity to learn many different techniques and broader aspects of the subject. What a delight!"

ETHEL Y. HOWEY, San Antonio, Texas. "Ai," My Mother.

Ethel sewed from childhood. As a young mother, living in Hawaii, she made a Hawaiian quilt. Quiltmaking, became the "meaningful hobby" that is both an avocation and a vocation. She teaches quiltmaking, designs, quilts, and judges quilt shows, finding the friendship and sharing the most satisfying aspect of quilts. The melding of traditional Japanese fabrics with traditional American quilt designs is a stylistic pursuit begun by Ethel several years ago. She plans to continue in this vein, finding it fulfilling because of her Japanese parentage and American upbringing.

ALICE HYDE, Des Moines, Iowa. Mother's Album Quilt.

"My love of needlework comes from my mother, but I discovered quilting on my own in the late 1970s. Quilting…my link to the past and my gift to the future. I am a lawyer for the Iowa Attorney General's Office, so quilting also provides a much-needed refuge." With her response to the needleartist's questionaire, Alice included a lengthy and beautiful explanation of the blocks, signatures, and symbolism in her quilt. Here are her notes on the "Pumper Truck block," delightful to see here, once again, so far beyond Baltimore: "Wreath Block Seven (bottom left) is signed by my youngest brother, Benjamin Clark. Benjamin's birthday is June 24, between Flag Day and Fourth of July, so I wanted something patriotic. Ben is a dedicated volunteer fireman and second assistant fire chief in our home town fire department. The old-fashioned fire pumper has "Adams" embroidered across it, for our home town of Adams, a small village in northern New York State. My mother and three of my brothers and sisters still live there, and two more live within 15 miles."

CLAIRE JARRATT, Pleasant Hill, California. Friendship.

Claire is a noted quiltmaking talent in her California community. She writes, "In the past I have taught hand piecing, crazy patch, some appliqué, and machine piecing. I enjoy quilting and do it almost every day."

FAYE LABANARIS (for The Good Ladies of Baltimore North and the Cocheco Quilters Guild), Dover, New Hampshire. Baltimore Friends.

"These blocks were the first bocks made by my first students. They no longer wanted these blocks because 'their colors changed,' or they didn't like the block. These 'orphaned blocks' found a home around a traditional Baltimore basket done in contemporary colors. One basic group of ladies has been together for Baltimore classes for over four years. They are the Good Ladies of Baltimore North. To date, there are over 200 members." Faye has talent, charm, a kind heart, and a fairly phenomenal following of quiltmakers who take her classes in Maine, Vermont, and New Hampshire. Into her full life (she is the mother of two boys) she squeezes research into Hawaiian quilts, science curriculum consulting for her school district, and professional quiltmaking. A lush commision piece, a Baltimore-style wall quilt, sports its sculptured roses in *Dimensional Appliqué—Baskets, Blooms, and Baltimore Borders.*

KATHERINE L. MCKEARN, Towson, Maryland. Allegheny Avenue Album.

"I've been making my original design quilts since 1991 and have exhibited in many national shows and won lots of awards. [This quilt] reflects the chaos of life with a husband, three young kids, a dog, and an old house. I feel like I'm in constant tug-of-war between all that and my quiltmaking!"

RUTH MEYERS, Dhahran, Saudi Arabia and Exmore, Virginia. Hearts and Birds.

Ruth is a prodigious, talented, internationally recognized artist whose medium is quiltmaking. Her themes are wide-ranging, some of the most evocative being those inspired by the Moslem culture of Saudi Arabia where she lives most of the year. Among this year's quilts is a silk one, each of whose exquisite floral blocks she designed, drew, and painted, then quilted. A needleartist for this series, she completed an elegant border during the air raids of Desert Storm, and has, for the past two summers, graciously set earlier blocks from the *Baltimore Beauties* series into three tops that, quilted, debut in *Volume III*. To my knowledge, Ruth is the sole contemporary professional quiltmaker who has handmade a full-sized (twenty-five block) complexly floral vine-bordered Baltimore-style Album Quilt on commission.

DIANNE MILLER, Attleboro, Massachusetts. Amour Galore.

"An artist all my life, I began quilting in 1985. While my original hand appliquéd pictorial designs have been recognized with numerous regional and national awards, this particular Album Quilt—begun under the tutelage of Louisa Smith, my teacher and friend—has been one of the most challenging and rewarding appliqué quilts I've ever had."

MARLENE PETERMAN, West Hills, California. Love Conquers All. Appliqué an Heirloom. Spring Basket.

Growing up in Scotland, Marlene learned to sew, knit, and crochet but did not quilt until she came to live in the United States. She now teaches and lectures nationwide on her favorite type of quilts—appliqué. Marlene is a well-loved teacher, soft-spoken and quite radiant, like her quilts.

ELLEN B. PETERS, Laconia, New Hampshire. Grapevine Lyre. Fleur-de-Lis. Sweetheart Rose Lyre. Crown of Laurel. Feather-Wreathed Heart.

Enthusiastic, energetic, helpful, and talented, Ellen is the quintessential teacher. "I graduated as an art teacher and tried many different arts before settling on quilting as the one I enjoyed the most. I am now an elementary teacher and teach quilting to my students; during the summer I teach adults to quilt." I first met Ellen at the Vermont Quilt Festival and have appreciated her friendship ever since. Her work appears in *Appliqué 12 Easy Ways!* and in *Baltimore Beauties, Volume III.*

JUDY PLEISS, Indianapolis, Indiana. Memories of Love and Caraway Cookies.

"I have been sewing, knitting, and embroidering since a small child, and a quiltmaker since 1976. I thrive on the challenge of creating my own variations of designs, however primitive, rather than using someone else's pattern. As a past president of the Quilters Guild of Indianapolis and a member of three quilt clubs, I find that these are my special friendships."

ARNOLD H. SAVAGE, Avon, Ohio. Baltimore-style Presentation Quilt Opus 50.

Several of the blocks in this quilt are original designs by the maker, but most of them are based on research from currently available books—"William Rush Dunton's book being of great help." This quilt, unique in its rectangular block design, was designed and executed as a special wedding quilt for Arnold's cousin and his bride. Full of symbolism, it was completed in just over six weeks. "The center block is the well house at Indiana University where the couple was engaged, which is a tradition on the campus. The crossed flags are those of Indiana on the left and Indiana University on the right." A wonderful explanatory description accompanied this quilt and noted the fact that its unveiling after his cousin's wedding ceremony brought a roar of applause from the seated guests, and tears of astonishment from the bride.

CAROL A. SPALDING, Oakhurst, California. Floral Miniature.

After years of drawing and painting, Carol, an award-winning artist, turned to the medium of fiber art. She applied her artistic ability first to piecing fabric and then turned to traditional appliqué and *Broderie Perse*, where she found more freedom of expression. In her approach to fiber art, Carol intermingles different techniques, patterns, and colors. She seeks to imitate in fabric various forms and shapes from nature.

CHERYL A. SPENCE, Carmel, Indiana. Twenty-fifth Anniversary.

"Although I have been a quiltmaker for some 20 years, this was my first hand appliqué undertaking. I'm so glad our Charm Club presented an album challenge because I thoroughly enjoyed it. I'm especially pleased that my father, Henry J. Schaefer, did all the embroidery detail for the blocks and I added the inking." And I'm pleased to have Cheryl here in the *Baltimore Beauties* series. She and fellow Charm Club member, Pamela Reising, were my Houston Quilt Market bosom buddies, for years on end, more than a decade ago when she owned a quilt shop, Pam was Director of Marketing for Mountain Mist, and I owned a mail-order business. How nice still to be quilting together.

PATRICIA L. STYRING, St. Augustine, Florida. Baltimore Album Nouveau with Angels.

"I have been sewing since childhood and have quilted seven years. I appliqué almost exclusively in both traditional and very contemporary forms. Using freezer paper and a glue-stick, I paste all elements of a design together to preview the finished block or border, then I appliqué. Every moment of this quilt was a joy. I was sorry when it was done!" Patricia notes that the house is her home, the angels, border, and fuchsias (in the right-hand cornucopia) are also original, and the tree has berries with her family members' names on them.

SHIRLEY TICKLE, Terrey Hills, N.S.W., Australia. Grandeur.

"My interest in Baltimore quilts began after reading an article by Elly in *Quilter's Newsletter Magazine*. Then I purchased *Baltimore Beauties and Beyond* and *Spoken Without a Word*, which I just love. My quilt is queen size (floor to floor) and took about 1,222 hours to make. My teacher was Margaret Sampson of Sydney; she teaches at "The Quilting Bee" patchwork shop in Gordon, Sydney. I attended ten lessons and completed one block every two weeks."

Appendix I:
Quilt Shop Festivities and
Classroom Courses

The following descriptions of possible quilting classes use *Design a Baltimore Album Quilt!* as a textbook. Anyone who would like to teach these course formats or who would like to use these descriptions and materials lists verbatim has the author's and the publisher's permission to do so.

A. TWO QUILT SHOP EVENING FESTIVITIES

1. **Come to a Baltimore Album Reunion!** All of our customers are welcome to this private evening shop opening. We particularly encourage fans of the *Baltimore Beauties* series. If you've worked from the series, bring your blocks! If you're interested in starting an Album Quilt on your own, or signing up for one of our classes, come. You'll hear enthusiastic reports of how much fun and how unexpectedly easy working on this once-in-a-lifetime heirloom can be. We'll have a "special price" table of all the supplies (beyond books and fabric) that make work on these quilts even easier. **Shop set-up:** Have all the *Baltimore Beauties* books available. During show-and-tell, have the maker point out which book she used. Have a listing, sign-up sheet, and handout on all your upcoming Baltimore classes. Have those classes' teachers give a five-minute presentation on each class during the reception. Serve refreshments and leave time to shop.

2. **Design a Baltimore Album Quilt! Book Party.** Not sure how to set your Baltimore Album-style Quilt together? Want more information on appliqué borders? Come meet *Design a Baltimore Album Quilt! A Teach-Yourself Course in Sets and Borders* by Elly Sienkiewicz. We'll give you an entertaining overview of Elly's book (including a round of Quilter's Solitaire), do a sample exercise from it, and familiarize you with the basics of classic Album Quilt sets and borders. Punch, cookies, and conversation included. **Materials:** Bring a pack of playing cards, pencil, paper scissors, repositionable glue-stick, and your copy of *Design a Baltimore Album Quilt!* Please bring any blocks you've done for show-and-tell, and your set and border thoughts and questions. (Note: Advertise upcoming shop classes at the party. The teacher for the six-week design class could display her fused mock-ups of a one-block-with-borders

wall quilt. Or, she could bring a fused Album top, "The Heart-Garlanded Album."

B. SIX-WEEK CLASS (six 2¹/2-hour classes)

Learn the Wonders of Baltimore-style Album Quilt Sets and Borders! Join this lively group in working through the eighteen lessons of *Design a Baltimore Album Quilt!* by Elly Sienkiewicz. Whether you just want to know these quilts better, or are already several blocks into your own Album, this course is for you. It introduces you to all those design elements you must consider in designing a dynamic set for your Album. Basic issues like sewing blocks, sashings, and borders together, making a Master Border Pattern to customize border fit and design, quilting, and special bindings are covered. And this is such an easy, information-packed class—no sewing required! Make an optional fused fabric piece (a frameable work of art when completed, or the top to a blanket-stitched wall quilt or miniature) to exhibit all you've learned. If you are all ready to design and make a border for a completed set of blocks, study with the class, but customize your border to your particular needs. **Materials for the first class:** Bring a pack of playing cards, pencil, paper scissors, repositionable glue-stick, and your copy of *Design a Baltimore Album Quilt!* Thereafter, bring the supplies listed in the "Getting Started" section of the book. Bring your other *Baltimore Beauties* books to refer to.

Note to the Teacher: Every instructor has a different style; the following very sketchy class schedule is simply a suggestion to help you formulate an exciting class with your own signature on it: **1st Week:** Quilter's Solitaire, "Picture This" discussions, first lesson. Homework: Sign up to do one (more if you care to) of Lessons 2, 3, or 4 to present for a few minutes of class discussion next week. **2nd Week:** Blocks. Present the technical information (pin up models for discussion, using blocks you and the class have already made). Break the lessons up for study teams to do in small groups, then present to the class. Homework: Begin your class model. Choose one block (or your choice set) to make a fabric mock-up of. Prepare its fabric for fusing; cut out the motifs. You will be bordering this in Lesson 17 and can pace the project. Be ready to focus on borders for it in the 4th week. (Refer to *Appliqué 12 Easy Ways!* for fused appliqué with a hand blanket-stitch finish (or machine satin stitch). The potential beauty of these fused models is so great that some will prefer to do them on background fabric, rather than paper.) **3rd**

Week: Medallions and Sashings. **4th and 5th Weeks:** Borders. **6th Week:** Celebration, presentation of fused pictures, miniatures, or wall quilt tops.

C. ONCE-A-MONTH AFTERNOON OR EVENING CLASS (Six to ten months)

Album Masters Class. Add the support of the group to finishing your Album! This monthly get-together is run as an encouragement and problem-solving seminar for people who are at least four blocks into their Album Quilt. The format is informal and designed to address your needs. Additional new techniques/sources/ideas will be shared by class members who will sign up and present something of particular interest pertaining to Baltimore Albums once a month on a rotating basis. (If you have lots of specific block styles you'd like to make, consider signing up as well for one of the courses listed in the Appendix to *Baltimore Album Quilts, Volume I, Pattern Companion*.) In recognition of the group's importance in the classic quilts, our "Album Masters class" will be offered repeatedly as long as its members wish to see it continue, and new members wish to join.

D. YEAR-LONG CLASS (of 2½- to 3-hour classes)

Make the Most Romantic of Album Quilts Yours: The Heart-Garlanded Album. Stitch a full-sized Album reproduction with us. Have fun, learn tons, and get this priceless quilt top done! You'll make your very own reproduction of the classic white/green/red (with flashes of blue doves) mid-nineteenth-century Album from the Brooklyn Museum of Art's collection. (See page 8 in *Volume II*. Complete patterns for the whole quilt—both full-size and miniature—are in *Design a Baltimore Album Quilt! A Teach-Yourself Course in Sets and Borders*, also by Elly Sienkiewicz.) If you prefer, make this quilt in miniature (shown on that book's back cover)—or do both! We welcome all approaches: needleturn appliqué, fused appliqué with a buttonhole finish, machine appliqué, and either full-sized or miniature—or both. This is an intermediate class for those who have had an appliqué class, or some experience doing appliqué. **Materials for the first class:** Bring your red, green, and blue accent (for the dove) to class. (Note: The original doves are red.) Bring fabric from your stash, but put off buying new until we talk a bit about fabric selection for this predominantly red and green on white quilt. You'll see that there will be many "moods" possible in the class's reds and greens. Bring freezer paper, pencil, stapler, paper scissors, repositionable tape, and your copy of *Design a Baltimore Album Quilt!* We'll discuss fabric, techniques, pace of the schedule, and trace off our patterns in this first class.

Note to the Teacher: Consider patterning your block approach to the lesson order of *Volume I*, taking one technique per class. Except for the elegantly embroidered center one, the blocks repeat. You may want to teach mock hand appliqué from Harriet Hargrave's *Mastering Machine Appliqué* for some parts of a block or the border. Invite a class member or guest teacher to share for that session if this method is not familiar to you. If possible, meeting every second or third week would help keep the class on a reasonable production schedule.

Appendix II: Sources

The following sources for items mentioned in the text may be of interest to readers.

Betty Alderman, 67 Glenwood Boulevard, Mansfield, OH 44906. Betty has several appliqué patterns available for purchase. The full border for her "Family Album" costs $12.50 including shipping.

Karen Bludorn, 3863 Laura Lane, Erlanger, KY 41018. Karen sells her patterns for the border and her original blocks in "Dances with Flowers." Send a large SASE for information.

Country House Cottons, Kim and Milly Churbuck, Box 375, Fayette, IA 52142. Send a large SASE for ordering information on carefully graded hand-dyed 100% cottons, hand-drawn Baltimore Album Quilt labels, or hand-customized fabric and label orders, tailored to your needs.

Judy Severson, Inc., P.O. Box 285, Lake Mills, WI 53551. Judy is a printmaker whose embossed prints, posters, and notecards are inspired by traditional American quilt patterns. Her original prints are done by hand on an old etching press. Her work is available at fine stores in the U.S. and abroad. For ordering information, send a large SASE.

About the Author

For ten years now Elly Sienkiewicz has been honing her expertise on the Baltimore Album Quilt style of the mid-nineteenth century. Combining old loves—history, religion, art, and needlework—these quilts have become for Elly and thousands like her, "The Fascinating Ladies of Bygone Baltimore."

The Victorian Album Quilt genre itself has gained increasing prominence in the decade Elly has been studying it. Its appeal to major collectors and investors is the stuff of headlines and feature articles. Most impressively, it brings immense pleasure to those who, in the late twentieth century, ply their needles in this expressive style. The question of why these quilts have such broad appeal, such intense holding power, is addressed by Elly in her *Baltimore Beauties* series. With a connoisseur's enthusiasm, she probes the artistic, technical, historic, and philosophical depths of these antebellum appliqué Albums.

Elly's other books include the phenomenally popular *Appliqué 12 Easy Ways! Charming Quilts, Giftable Projects, and Timeless Techniques*. That book's broad appeal may even be surpassed by her upcoming book, *Appliqué a Paper Greeting! 50 Inexpensive, Easy-to-Make Cards and Gifts for Crafters of All Ages*. This charming book, too, reflects Elly's fondness for the Victorian decorative mode and warmth of written expression.

A sewer from childhood, Elly's love of quilts and her initial instruction in making them came from those West Virginia relatives whom she has visited with a comforting regularity all of her life. Degrees from Wellesley College and the University of Pennsylvania led to a teaching career (history, social studies, and English) before staying at home with her three young children. Pursuing a number of entrepreneurial endeavors from home, she eventually taught quiltmaking and for seven years ran a mail-order quilt supply business. Already in some demand from her first book, *Spoken Without a Word*, Elly took a brief respite from teaching and lecturing to become a tour guide for historic Washington, D.C. Refreshed and reinspired, she began to research, write, design, teach, and lecture again—a mode she's continued in happily ever since. Elly lives in Washington with her husband, Stan, and their children, Donald, Alex, and Katya.

Books by Elly Sienkiewicz

With the exception of her first, self-published, book, all Elly's books are available from C & T Publishing, P.O. Box 1456, Lafayette, California, 94549. Telephone: 1-800-284-1114

- *Spoken Without a Word—A Lexicon of Selected Symbols, with 24 Patterns from Classic Baltimore Album Quilts* (published by the author in 1983)

- *Baltimore Beauties and Beyond, Studies in Classic Album Quilt Appliqué, Volume I* (1989)

- *Baltimore Album Quilts, Historic Notes and Antique Patterns—A Pattern Companion to Baltimore Beauties and Beyond, Studies in Classic Album Quilt Appliqué, Volume I* (1990)

- *Baltimore Beauties and Beyond, Studies in Classic Album Quilt Appliqué, Volume II* (1991)

- *Appliqué 12 Easy Ways! Charming Quilts, Giftable Projects, and Timeless Techniques* (1991)

- *Design a Baltimore Album Quilt! A Teach-Yourself Course in Sets and Borders* (1992)

- *Dimensional Appliqué—Baskets, Blooms, and Baltimore Borders—A Pattern Companion to Baltimore Beauties and Beyond, Studies in Classic Album Quilt Appliqué, Volume II* (1993)

- *Baltimore Beauties and Beyond, Studies in Classic Album Quilt Appliqué, Volume III* (1993)

- *Baltimore Revival! Historic Quilts in the Making* (1994)

Other Fine Quilting Books from C&T Publishing

An Amish Adventure, Roberta Horton
The Art of Silk Ribbon Embroidery, Judith Montano
Boston Commons Quilt, Blanche Young and
     Helen Young Frost
Calico and Beyond, Roberta Horton
A Celebration of Hearts, Jean Wells and Marina Anderson
Christmas Traditions From the Heart, Margaret Peters
Crazy Quilt Handbook, Judith Montano
Crazy Quilt Odyssey, Judith Montano
Fans, Jean Wells
Fine Feathers, Marianne Fons
Flying Geese Quilt, Blanche Young and Helen Young Frost
Friendship's Offering, Susan McKelvey
Happy Trails, Pepper Cory
Heirloom Machine Quilting, Harriet Hargrave
Imagery on Fabric, Jean Ray Laury
Irish Chain Quilt, Blanche Young and Helen Young Frost
Isometric Perspective, Katie Pasquini-Masopust
Landscapes & Illusions, Joen Wolfrom
Let's Make Waves, Marianne Fons and Liz Porter
Light and Shadows, Susan McKelvey
The Magical Effects of Color, Joen Wolfrom
Mariner's Compass, Judy Mathieson
Mastering Machine Appliqué, Harriet Hargrave
Memorabilia Quilting, Jean Wells

New Lone Star Handbook, Blanche Young and
     Helen Young Frost
Perfect Pineapples, Jane Hall and Dixie Haywood
Picture This, Jean Wells and Marina Anderson
Plaids and Stripes, Roberta Horton
PQME Series: Milky Way Quilt, Jean Wells
PQME Series: Nine-Patch Quilt, Jean Wells
PQME Series: Pinwheel Quilt, Jean Wells
PQME Series: Stars & Hearts Quilt, Jean Wells
Quilting Designs from Antique Quilts, Pepper Cory
Quilting Designs from the Amish, Pepper Cory
Story Quilts, Mary Mashuta
Trip Around the World Quilts, Blanche Young and
     Helen Young Frost
Visions: The Art of the Quilt, Quilt San Diego
Visions: Quilts of a New Decade, Quilt San Diego
Working in Miniature, Becky Schaefer
Wearable Art for Real People, Mary Mashuta
3 Dimensional Design, Katie Pasquini

For more information, write for a free catalog:
C & T Publishing
P.O. Box 1456
Lafayette, CA 94549
(1-800-284-1114)

C & T Publishing Announces...

Revivalist Baltimore-Style Album Quilt Contest and Exhibition
This contest will result in a traveling exhibit to appear first in April 1994 at Rita Barber's Quilter's Heritage Celebration in Lancaster, Pennsylvania. For entry forms, write to C & T Publishing's Great Revivalist Baltimore-Style Album Quilt Contest, C & T Publishing, P.O.Box 1456, Lafayette, CA 94549.

Call for Teacher Honors
A book is planned to celebrate the 1994 show of contemporary Baltimore-style Album Quilts. In that book, we'd like to honor the many teachers of the Baltimore style who have made it bloom so gloriously once again in their region of the country and of the world. If you would like to nominate a teacher for this recognition, please send the teacher's name and address and a short note about the good job they have done. We'd like to hear how their teaching affected your work and the work of others in your area. Please include your own name and address and send it to C & T Publishing, Teacher Honors, P.O. Box 1456, Lafayette, CA 94549. Nominations should be received by August 1993.

Quilting Teachers Resources
Did you know that C & T Publishing has great resources for teachers? We'd like to give teachers support. We can send lesson plans, contest news, new book announcements, trunk show information, book reviews, seminar news, and other updates. Send your name, address, and phone number to C & T Publishing. Why not include a "Wish List" letting us know what you feel we could do for you as a quilt teacher. We value your input.